Preparing for Graduate Study in Psychology

D0190378

PREPARING FOR

Graduate Study in Psychology

101

Questions and Answers

Second edition

William Buskist, *Auburn University*
Caroline Burke, *Carleton College*

Blackwell
Publishing

BLACKWELL PUBLISHING
350 Main Street, Malden, MA 02148-5020, USA
9600 Garsington Road, Oxford OX4 2DQ, UK
550 Swanston Street, Carlton, Victoria 3053, Australia

First edition published 1996 by Allyn & Bacon as William R. Buskist and
Thomas R. Sherburne, *Preparing for Graduate Study in Psychology*

This second edition published 2007 by Blackwell Publishing Ltd

1   2007

Library of Congress Cataloging-in-Publication Data

ISBN-13: 978-1-4051-4052-2 (paperback)
ISBN-10: 1-4051-4052-6 (paperback)

A catalogue record for this title is available from the British Library.

Set in 10/12pt Sabon
by Graphicraft Limited, Hong Kong

The publisher's policy is to use permanent paper from mills that operate
a sustainable forestry policy, and which has been manufactured from pulp
processed using acid-free and elementary chlorine-free practices. Furthermore,
the publisher ensures that the text paper and cover board used have met
acceptable environmental accreditation standards.

For further information on
Blackwell Publishing, visit our website:
www.blackwellpublishing.com

For psychology majors everywhere – may your intelligence, curiosity, sheer determination and hard work lead you to much accomplishment and distinction.

Contents

Preface

Combined, the two of us have been teaching psychology for over thirty years. During that time, we have taught thousands of undergraduates, many of whom have had strong desires to attend graduate school in psychology. Because none of these students had ever applied to graduate school before, they naturally had plenty of questions about how to go about the application process. This book is a direct result of those questions – what we have compiled is a long list of the most common questions and their answers – 101 of them – that we've been asked over the years about "how to get into graduate school in psychology."

At the very outset let us be clear about one thing: getting into graduate school is nothing like getting into undergraduate school. It is not like one day you decide you want to go to graduate school, so you send away for application forms, fill them out, mail them away with a check, and voila – you're in!

Getting into graduate school is not simple. Being accepted into a graduate program in psychology generally requires a large investment of time, highly efficient organizational skills, and a lot of good old-fashioned legwork. In addition, depending on the schools to which you're applying, the process can be highly competitive. Thus, our goal for writing this book is to help you become better prepared to apply to graduate school in psychology.

How This Book is Organized

The book is divided into two basic parts. The first part contains questions that our undergraduate students have asked us about graduate school over the past years. A brief, to-the-point answer is provided for each of these questions. These answers are intended to put you into contact with the "basics" involved in gathering information about graduate programs, applying to them, interviewing at them, and making sense of how graduate admissions committees might evaluate your credentials relative to their programs. In answering these questions, we relied on our own experiences with the application process, the insights of first-year graduate students who recently and successfully completed this process, and the collective wisdom of several faculty colleagues who are highly experienced with graduate admissions procedures.

The second part of the book is devoted to a series of appendices aimed at helping you do the paperwork and jumping through all of the hoops involved in applying to graduate school in psychology. We have provided a timetable for completing your preparations, a description of the different concentrations in psychology, an outline for preparing your vita and a sample vita, and three sample letters of intent. Finally, this part of the book also contains other sources of information you may wish to consult during your preparation for graduate study and a glossary of terms related to graduate school and the application process. We also have included a wealth of Internet resources for you to consult during the application process.

How to Use This Book

This book can read in a few hours and used for consulting throughout the application process. It may be used as a regular textbook; however, it is best utilized as a handy reference tool, first as way of becoming familiar with the application process, and then for consulting as you go through the application process.

Although the text itself is chockfull of useful information, you may also find the material contained in the appendices very handy at the outset of the application process. The timetable in Appendix I will help you organize and develop your personal strategy for how best to use your time to start – and finish – the application process. The outline for writing your vita found in Appendix III will help you organize your personal academic data in one central location, which will be very handy for you to consult as you fill out application after application. You should also read through the three sample letters of intent (personal statements) in Appendix IV before you sit down to write your own letter of intent so that you will have a solid understanding the structure and content of this essay.

Of course, you will also find the other materials at the end of the book helpful in familiarizing yourself with the language and subfields of psychology that are directed towards graduate school in general and graduate school in psychology in particular. We've also included a far-ranging and annotated list of other sources you may find useful in the application process.

A Favor, Please

We would like to know your reaction to our book. If you have a question that is not answered in the book, a suggestion for making the book more useful to other students, a comment, good, bad, or otherwise relating to your experience with this book, we would like to hear from you. You can write us at the addresses given below. Thank you and best wishes for success in graduate school – we wish you the very best in your pursuit of graduate study in psychology!

Dr. Bill Buskist   Dr. Caroline Burke
Psychology Department   Psychology Department
Auburn University   Carleton College
Auburn, AL 36849-5214   Northfield, MN 55057
buskiwf@auburn.edu   cburke@carleton.edu

Acknowledgments

We thank our many undergraduate students for raising the questions and the issues we explore in this book. We also thank Chris Cardone and Sarah Coleman at Blackwell Publishing for their excellent behind-the-scenes work in making it possible to put this book in the hands of so many capable students.

Chapter 1
Introduction:
The Big Picture

Before applying to graduate programs, you should be generally knowledgeable about graduate schools and psychology graduate programs: how they are organized and function, their admission criteria, the kinds of specialties and degrees they offer, degree requirements, and so on. Having such knowledge puts you in a sound position from which to make decisions about your qualifications for graduate school, the kinds of professional interests you may wish to pursue, and the kind of work you ultimately may wish to do. The questions and answers presented in this chapter are intended to provide you with general information on these issues and to help you better understand the different kinds of goals you may accomplish during your graduate school career.

Q1. What is the difference between a graduate school and a graduate program?

A1. A graduate school is an administrative body, usually directed by a dean, which establishes general admission criteria and other policies relating to all the graduate programs within a particular college or university. A graduate program is a group of faculty members that is organized around a particular subfield or subdiscipline, such as a graduate program in clinical psychology or a graduate program in developmental psychology. The graduate program may establish its own admission criteria, policies, and deadlines, so long as they are consistent with the graduate school's criteria, policies, and deadlines (graduate programs often have more rigorous acceptance criteria than graduate schools). At many colleges and universities, the application for a particular graduate program is submitted to the graduate school. At other colleges and universities, there may be no centralized graduate school, so the application is submitted directly to the academic department in which the particular graduate program resides. When the application is complete (application form, letter of intent, Graduate Record Examination (GRE) scores, transcripts, letters of recommendation, and other materials) the application is then forwarded to the appropriate graduate program. Admission to a graduate program requires that you meet the acceptance criteria of both the graduate school and graduate program.

Q2. How difficult is it to get into graduate school? What kind of grade point average (GPA) do I need in order to be competitive for being accepted into graduate school?

A2. Graduate programs always seek the best students they can get. Acceptance to graduate programs is extremely competitive, especially to those with highly regarded PhD training (clinical programs have among the most stringent entrance requirements). Some of these programs may receive as many as 300 or 400 applications each year but accept only 3 or 4 individuals. In these cases, the typical overall GPA of the accepted students may be in the 3.8 to 4.0 range and the typical GRE score may be in the 1300 plus range. Other PhD programs are less competitive, although the typical GPA of their students is still fairly high, in the 3.3 to 3.5 range. If your GPA is lower than this range, you may wish to consider applying to Master's programs, which are typically less competitive in terms of their entrance requirements. If you are able to perform at the "A" level in a Master's program, you are then in an improved position to apply for, and be accepted into, a PhD program.

Q3. How soon should I start preparing for my graduate training?

A3. Because your overall GPA is a major factor that most graduate schools and programs take into consideration when accepting students for graduate work, you really should begin preparing for graduate school during your freshman year. However, becoming involved in research projects and other relevant activities should begin to take place during your sophomore and junior years. Waiting until your senior year to participate in research projects will not do you much good because you will begin the actual application process during the fall term of that year. A complete timetable of the preparation process is given in Appendix I.

Q4. When should I send away for application materials for the graduate programs to which I wish to apply?

A4. You should write away for application materials no later than September of your senior year. The easiest way to request application materials is to e-mail departments to which you wish to apply. If you wait much longer than September, especially considering the time it takes to process your request, you may not be able to assemble your application package soon enough to meet some of the earlier deadlines (January 1). Writing away for application materials much earlier than September may not guarantee your earlier receipt of them, because many schools print new application forms each summer and they may not be available until the early fall months.

Q5. Are there any factors that can offset, or compensate for, a low GPA?

A5. The main factor that can offset a low GPA is high GRE (Graduate Record Examination) scores. If you have a modest GPA (e.g., a 3.2) but high GRE scores (1200 plus), a strong letter of intent, strong clinical or research experience, and strong letters of recommendation, you are likely to have a competitive application at many graduate schools. However, even very high GRE scores cannot compensate for having a low GPA, a mediocre letter of intent, and weak letters of recommendation.

Similarly, low GRE scores can be partially offset by a high GPA, a strong letter of intent, strong clinical or research experience, and strong letters of recommendation. Likewise, even very high GPA scores cannot compensate for having low GRE scores, a mediocre letter of intent, and weak letters of recommendation.

Q6. Is there a way that I can insure my acceptance to graduate school? Are there any short-cuts to getting into graduate school?

A6. There are no short-cuts to being accepted into graduate school. The main criteria are academic merit and evidence of intellectual potential. Both of these requirements can only be fulfilled through steadfast, thoughtful work during your undergraduate career. Membership in Psi Chi* (the national honor society for psychology students) or volunteer work at your local crisis center or participation in other extracurricular activities will not compensate for weak GRE scores. Instead, these factors may help graduate admissions committees to distinguish among applicants with equally impressive numbers (GPA and GRE scores).

*Requirements for becoming a member of Psi Chi include:

- Completion of 3 semesters or 5 quarters of college.
- Completion of 9 semester hours or 14 quarter hours of psychology courses
- Ranking in the top 35 percent of their class in general scholarship.
- Have a minimum GPA of 3.0 (on a 4.0 scale) in both psychology classes and in cumulative grades.

For more information about Psi Chi go to http://www.psichi.org

Q7. How long will it take me to earn my graduate degree?

A7. The pace at which you complete your graduate degree depends on the degree you are seeking and numerous personal factors, such as motivation, workload, specific degree requirements, and so on. In general, two years are needed to complete most Master's programs and four to six years to complete most PhD programs. There are some Master's programs that are designed to be completed in one year and others that combine both baccalaureate and graduate work for earning the Master's degree. Programs in clinical or counseling psychology generally require students to complete four years of coursework and then complete a one-year clinical internship before being awarded the PhD or PsyD degree (see also Q & A 23; for practical purposes, we will generally refer only to the PhD degree throughout the remainder of the book).

Note: Earning a degree in clinical or counseling psychology does not qualify an individual to practice psychology. Before an individual can practice (as in establishing a private practice for the purpose of providing therapy), he or she must have earned a degree in clinical or counseling psychology and pass a national licensure examination (and some states require the individual to pass additional requirements in order practice psychology in his or her particular state).

Although all graduate programs are designed to be completed within a specific time interval, the actual time it takes a graduate student to complete his or her course of study is often much longer. It is not uncommon for graduate students to take 6, 7, or even 8 years to complete what was supposed to be a four-year doctoral program. Major impediments to earning graduate degrees in a timely manner (or at all) include financial problems, competing interests, family commitments, problems in the graduate student major professor relationship, failure to settle on a thesis or dissertation topic, procrastination, and unfocused or ever-changing educational and career goals.

Q8. What is a terminal Master's degree?

A8. A terminal Master's degree is a Master's degree that is awarded in graduate programs designed for students who will not be continuing on toward their PhD. The term also applies to Master's degrees awarded from graduate programs that award only Master's degrees. However, just because you earn a terminal Master's degree does not mean that you cannot or should not apply to PhD or PsyD programs.

Q9. What is a "fifth-year program"?

A9. A fifth-year program may be one of two things. At some schools, a fifth-year program is a graduate program in which you may earn both a Bachelor's degree and a Master's degree by adding one year to the time it would normally take you to complete your Bachelor's degree. During this year, you would take graduate level courses centered on a single discipline, such as psychology, and possibly complete a major research project. At other schools, a fifth-year program is a graduate program in which you may earn a Master's degree in one year. Fifth-year programs have become popular alternatives to the traditional two-year Master's program, especially in schools of education.

Q10. What is a clinical internship?

A10. After clinical or counseling students have completed their coursework and other requirements of their particular PhD or PsyD program, they are required to complete a one-year off-campus internship in which they gain first-hand experience providing mental health care to individuals. Settings for the internship include mental health facilities, medical centers, hospitals (including Veterans Administration [VA] hospitals), prisons, and mental institutions. Clinical or counseling students must apply a year in advance to several sites at which they desire to intern. Like entrance to graduate school, acceptance at these sites is highly competitive – not all applicants are accepted into an internship program. In addition, internship sites are often located away from campus, which almost always involves the graduate student relocating, sometimes to locations across the country.

Q11. Do I need to know which area of psychology I am going to specialize in when I apply to graduate programs?

A11. If you are considering PhD programs, the answer is yes. PhD programs are generally organized around a specific subject area, such as social psychology, child clinical psychology, or sport psychology. The more you know about what it is you want to do with your career, the better off you will be when it comes to conveying your interests to admissions committees. Knowing the area (or areas) of psychology in which you wish to specialize demonstrates that you have already spent time thinking about the directions you wish your career to take. Professors reviewing your application will appreciate knowing that you have done your homework on career options in psychology: They favor applicants who know generally what they want for their careers and who can communicate this knowledge clearly in their letter of intent.

Q12. How many different concentrations or subfields of psychology are offered in graduate school?

A12. A tremendous variety of concentrations are available to graduate students in psychology. Virtually any aspect of human or nonhuman behavior is represented in graduate school, depending, of course, on the particular program to which you apply. Appendix II lists and defines some of the more common major concentrations of study represented in graduate programs today.

Q13. What is the difference between clinical psychology and counseling psychology?

A13. Clinical psychology and counseling psychology are closely related. In some graduate programs both clinical and counseling students share coursework and clinical work in common. It is typically the emphasis that differs between the two. Clinical psychology focuses more specifically on abnormal behavior and pathology and counseling psychology tends to focus more on normal development and wellness. Graduate students in each field must complete an APA-approved internship in order to receive a PhD. (Students must apply to internship sites late in their graduate careers, typically after their coursework is completed. However, although many graduate students have completed their dissertations before they go off on internship, many do not – completion of the dissertation is not a requirement for applying for internship at most schools.) Both counseling and clinical psychologists work in professional settings that treat a large variety of people: people with "everyday" more typical concerns and people who suffer with mental illness and/or other health-related disorders that interfere with everyday functioning.

Q14. If I am interested in working as a helping professional, is clinical/counseling psychology my only choice for graduate study?

A14. No, there are many kinds of fields of helping professionals, most of which do not require a PhD in clinical psychology, such as social work, psychiatric social work, school psychology, family and marital therapy, art therapy, play therapy, occupational therapy, or special education. Given the competitive nature of getting into a clinical or counseling psychology program, these professions represent good alternatives when contemplating a career in the helping professions.

Q15. What sorts of jobs are available for people who earn a Bachelor's degree in psychology and who wish to postpone going to graduate school for a year or more?

A15. Employment possibilities include the following: working for crisis centers, specialized shelters, substance abuse programs, nursing homes, mental health centers, mental retardation centers, medical centers, hospitals, and group homes (homes in which several persons, who have developmental disabilities, live under the immediate supervision of a specially trained helping professional). Salaries at these sorts of jobs are generally quite low, but the practical experience and career insights you gain may prove to be invaluable to you as you pursue graduate education in psychology. Faculty in your psychology department are likely to be well aware of job openings in these settings; consult them if you are looking for such a position. You should also feel free to contact these employers directly by phoning or e-mailing them.

Q16. What kind of jobs in psychology are available with a Master's degree?

A16. Many types of jobs are available to students who hold a Master's degree. Examples include: teaching at junior and community colleges, counseling under the supervision of a PhD in clinical or counseling psychology, working as a psychiatric aide at a mental health facility, working in private industry as a personnel manager, working in or supervising a mental health facility for persons with developmental disabilities, supervising group homes, working in special shelters and programs, and serving as an industrial or mental health consultant.

You may find that for the type or work and career you have chosen, you only need Master's-level training: there may be no pressing need to go on for a PhD. However, you should keep an open mind when it comes to graduate training. Often, training at the PhD level opens up more interesting and financially rewarding career options.

Q17. Should I earn my Master's degree first or go for my PhD immediately?

A17. It depends. Some PhD programs require that you obtain a Master's degree on your way to earning your PhD (these programs usually have a Master's program embedded within their PhD program). Other graduate programs do not have this requirement: You earn your PhD without first obtaining a Master's degree.

If you are unable to gain entry to a PhD program immediately after earning your baccalaureate degree, you may wish to apply to a Master's program (most likely to a terminal Master's program). Doing so will give you the opportunity to prove that you can do high quality graduate-level work in the classroom, and gain valuable research and teaching experience. If you are successful in your Master's program, you will then be in a more favorable position to be accepted into a PhD program.

Q18. What are the hurdles, or specific tasks, other than coursework, which I must accomplish in graduate school in order to obtain my PhD?

A18. Assuming that your graduate program involves getting a Master's degree on your way to obtaining your PhD, the sequence of non-coursework hurdles may look something like that which we describe below. (Keep in mind, of course, that specific programs will vary in the sorts of hurdles they present their students.)

- Completing your Master's thesis (which includes writing the proposal for your thesis, presenting your proposal before your thesis committee, conducting your proposed research, writing your thesis, and defending your write-up before your thesis committee).

- Satisfactorily completing the comprehensive or "preliminary" examinations. These exams cover the material presented in your coursework during your first two to three years of graduate school (although some programs schedule the comprehensive exams after the first year of coursework). These exams are usually each four to eight hours in length and may take up to a week to finish. (However, some programs give the comprehensive examination as a "take home" exam and will allow the student anywhere between a week and several weeks to complete it. This sort of comprehensive examination is generally much more rigorous than the comprehensive examinations that require students to sit in classroom for several hours answering shorter essay questions.) Passing the exams means that you will be allowed to move on in your program so as to pursue your PhD. In some graduate programs, failing the exams may mean that you must leave the program (usually after earning a terminal Master's degree); other programs allow graduate students an opportunity for remediation and a second crack at the exams. However, failing the comprehensive exam twice almost always guarantees expulsion from further graduate work in that program.
- It is possible to fail some of the exams without failing all of them. In this case, the graduate student is usually allowed to restudy and retake only the exams that he or she failed.
- Satisfactorily completing the oral examination that follows the comprehensive examination. The oral exam generally is given after passing the comprehensive examination but before being advanced to doctoral candidacy. The oral exam may last for as long as three hours and may cover the same topics as those covered by the comprehensive exam as well as other topics. As a general rule, any aspect of your coursework or research up to that point may be covered in the oral exam. The oral exam is given by your dissertation committee.
- In lieu of taking the comprehensive and oral examinations, some graduate programs give graduate students the opportunity to write a major area paper and present an oral defense over it. A major area paper is a comprehensive, integrated review paper covering a major area of psychological research. It is not uncommon for the major area paper to be in excess of 100 pages in length. Often, the topic discussed in the major area paper is closely related to the topic researched in the dissertation.
- Completing your doctoral dissertation (which includes writing the proposal for your dissertation, presenting your proposal before your

dissertation committee, conducting your proposed research, writing your dissertation, and defending your write-up before your dissertation committee).

Q19.   What is the difference between a thesis and a dissertation?

A19.   Both the thesis and the dissertation are written reports of independent research conducted by a graduate student. Completing a thesis generally is a requirement to earn a Master's degree; completing a dissertation is a requirement for completing the PhD. Although both should involve original research on the part of the graduate student, the dissertation is usually a longer, more detailed, and extensive report than the thesis. In most graduate programs, the steps involved in completing each are roughly the same:

- *Step 1*: Select a topic or small set of topics. Review the relevant empirical literature to develop your interests and knowledge of the topic and to develop ideas for your own research.
- *Step 2*: Once you have an idea for your research, prepare a thesis or dissertation proposal (containing a review of the literature, rationale for your study, description of the methods and procedures, description of how your data will be analyzed, a brief description of your predicted results, and the implications of your findings for what is known about the question you are studying).
- *Step 3*: Present the proposal to a committee consisting of your major professor and several other faculty, all of whom you have asked to serve on your thesis or dissertation committee.
- *Step 4*: After gaining the approval of your committee, conduct the research. Generally speaking, your committee will recommend revisions in your proposal, especially regarding your proposed research methodology.
- *Step 5*: Once the research is completed, analyze your data and write the report (following the same general approach as outlined in Step 2). Your report will be written under the close supervision of your major professor. Before the report is finished, your major professor will likely ask you to revise it several times.
- *Step 6*: Once your major professor has given the report his or her approval, schedule the defense meeting. Prior to the actual meeting, you will give each member of your committee a copy of your report to read. At the defense meeting, you will present your research to the committee. Even if the committee approves it, you will likely be asked to make revisions in the written report. If the committee fails

the report, you will be asked either to do the research and written report over again, or select a new topic and start from scratch.

Q20. What is a major professor?

A20. A major professor is a graduate faculty member who chairs a graduate student's thesis or dissertation committee. Graduate students generally work more closely with their major professor than they do other graduate faculty. Major professors are also sometimes called "major advisors" or "mentors."

Q21. Is it better to seek a Master's degree that has a thesis option than a Master's degree without a thesis option?

A21. If you are interested in going on for a PhD or other advanced degree beyond the Master's level, then you should seek acceptance in a Master's program that requires the thesis. Because most PhD programs are research oriented, they are looking for students who want to do research and who have an aptitude for it. PhD programs that accept a Master's-level student generally require that student to have completed a thesis. In cases where the student is coming without a thesis, the PhD program faculty often require the student to complete a research project equivalent to a thesis before being fully admitted into the PhD program.

Q22. If I get my Master's degree at one school, am I required to stay there to get my PhD or can I move to a different school?

A22. You are always free to transfer to another school so long as you are accepted to a program at that school. A primary advantage of getting both your Master's and PhD at the same school is efficiency: You don't need to spend precious time getting acquainted with a new campus, a new library, a new faculty, a new city, and so on. There is certain to be some "down" time when you move from one school to another. However, if your scholarly interests and academic needs change while you are earning your Master's degree, or if you are otherwise unhappy, then you should either look for a more suitable graduate program or discontinue your graduate study altogether. Remember, though, that if you do change schools, some of the credit for courses you took at the first school may not transfer to the second school. You'll likely have to take more courses if you change schools than if you stayed at just one.

Q23. What is the difference between a PhD and a PsyD?

A23. The PhD (Doctor of Philosophy) is generally considered to be a more rigorous and prestigious degree than the PsyD (Doctor of Psychology). Earning a PhD requires extensive research and analytical training in addition to training within a particular specialty area. Requirements for the PsyD generally focus more on clinical training and emphasize research experience less (although this aspect of the PsyD is now beginning to change some). The PsyD is generally sought by those individuals who wish only to practice psychology in a mental health or other therapeutic setting, such as private practice. Earning a PhD in clinical psychology provides a greater range of career opportunities in psychology in addition to private practice. These opportunities include: teaching at the college or university level, working in medical centers and mental health centers, working in industry, or for a governmental agency. The PsyD is usually offered by private or professional schools (although there are some exceptions) and are generally more expensive to earn than the PhD.

Q24. What are my career options with a PhD in psychology?

A24. Obtaining a PhD gives you more career options than obtaining only a Master's or baccalaureate degree, although at the Master's level there may be more jobs but at less pay. Depending upon your area of expertise, you may find employment in any of the following areas: College and university teaching, research, administration, consulting, governmental agencies, secondary schools, private practice as a clinician, and working as a teacher, researcher, or mental health service provider in medical centers, mental health facilities, governmental agencies, or industry.

Q25. What is the salary range for new PhDs in psychology?

A25. There is tremendous variety in the salary range for new PhDs. Those who get jobs at the college or university level as assistant professors generally start in the $45,000 to $60,000 range. Clinical psychologists or industrial/organizational psychologists who get jobs in business or engineering departments generally start at a higher salary. Those new PhDs who enter into private practice or into industry may start at a lower initial salary, but will generally make more money as their career develops. We know of a recent PhD from our clinical psychology program who started her first job in the low $80,000 range!

Q26. Will there be a job available for me after I complete my Master's degree or PhD in psychology?

A26. There is no guarantee that you will be able to find the job you desire by getting an advanced degree. The job market varies depending upon your qualifications, training, and experience in your area of specialization. There almost always seem to be more jobs available for applied psychologists than for research psychologists. The job market for clinical psychologists and industrial/organizational psychologists, in particular, always seems good.

To get a ballpark idea of the kinds of jobs currently available to people graduating with advanced degrees in psychology, you may wish to read the employment advertisement sections of the *Chronicle of Higher Education*, the *APA Monitor*, and the *APS Observer*. These publications may be available in your library, through the Internet, or from professors in your psychology department.

Chapter 2
Getting Started: Preparing for the Big Change

Applying to graduate school – and getting accepted – is not something that is accomplished on the spur of the moment. Indeed, because admission to graduate school in psychology is extremely competitive, the earlier you start, the more competitive your application will be. The questions and answers in this chapter focus on how (a) getting good grades in your undergraduate courses, (b) involvement in research, (c) publishing research reports, (d) participating in conference presentations, and (e) becoming a member of Psi Chi will strengthen your application to graduate school. This chapter also emphasizes the creation of a vita for documenting your participation in these activities.

Q27. What undergraduate classes are the most important ones to take for doing graduate work in psychology?

A27. Different graduate programs emphasize different aspects or concentrations within psychology. However, most graduate programs require students to complete a set of "core" classes, which are likely to include the following: history of psychology, research methods, statistics, neuroscience (often called "biopsychology" and sometimes "physiological psychology"), learning, cognitive psychology, sensation and perception, developmental psychology, social psychology, abnormal psychology, and personality. Having done well in these courses at the undergraduate level will not only strengthen your application, it will also provide you with valuable background information for doing well in the corresponding graduate-level courses.

Q28. What are the best choices for an undergraduate minor if I am planning to go to graduate school?

A28. The choice for an undergraduate minor (now called a "concentration" at some schools) depends on many factors, including the area in which you wish to specialize and whether you wish to acquire special skills at the undergraduate level. The choice of specialty area is a personal one; you should choose a minor that accents your career interests. For example, if you wish to become a child developmental psychologist or a child clinical psychologist, you may wish to minor in child and family development or a related area.

However, two skills key to becoming a successful graduate student are writing and statistical analysis, including the use of computer software packages. You may wish to focus on one or both of these areas for an undergraduate minor (by taking advanced writing courses from the English department and advanced statistics courses from your mathematics or statistics department). You should also keep in mind that more and more graduate programs are placing an emphasis on genetic and other biological variables that influence behavior. If you will be applying to biological or neuroscience-oriented programs, you may wish to minor in a relevant biological area. If you are applying to clinical programs, you may wish to minor in chemistry or pharmacology because clinical psychologists often provide therapy for individuals who are also receiving drug therapy from a psychiatrist. If you are applying to industrial/organizational psychology programs, you may wish to minor in a field related to business or business management.

Q29. What factors outside of GPA and GRE scores are the most influential in terms of developing the appropriate credentials for becoming a graduate student?

A29. In a survey conducted in the early 1990s, this question was put to clinical psychologists who served on admissions committees for their graduate programs.* The two most heavily weighted factors were letters of recommendation and research experience. Clinical psychologists are not unique in the emphasis they place on these two factors – many, if not most, faculty who serve on admissions committees feel similarly. (One of the best ways to obtain a good letter of recommendation is to become an undergraduate research assistant.)

*Source: Stoup, C. M., & Benjamin, L. T. (1992). Graduate study in psychology. *American Psychologist, 37,* 1186–1202.

Q30. In terms of increasing my chances of getting into graduate school, what are the best kinds of extracurricular activities in which to become involved as an undergraduate?

A30. There are many extracurricular activities in which undergraduates may become involved to strengthen their application, including becoming a member of Psi Chi, working on a crisis line, at different kinds of shelters (special organizations for persons who are dealing with problems, such as having been raped or battered), special youth camps, and mental health facilities.

However, one of the most useful experiences you can have as an undergraduate is to become involved in research with a faculty member. Research work will give you first-hand experience in conducting research and, in some cases, analyzing and writing up the results. If you are attending a college or university that has a graduate program in psychology, you may be able to contact graduate students from whom you can learn a great deal about what it is like to in graduate school. There is also the chance that, depending on the depth of your involvement in the research, your work will lead to a publication or conference presentation in which you are an author, which will strengthen your application to graduate school. If you become a competent undergraduate research assistant, it will also put you in a position to ask your faculty research supervisor for a letter of recommendation.

Although you may have participated in other activities as an undergraduate, such as those involved in being a member of a fraternity or sorority, admissions committees are more interested in your commitment to psychology as discipline and career choice. To most admissions committees, being president of a social organization may not be as impressive as presenting a poster or paper at a national psychology conference.

Q31. How can I get research experience as an undergraduate?

A31. The psychology department at your school probably offers an undergraduate course entitled "Research in Special Topics" or "Independent Study," which is designed to give undergraduates an opportunity to become involved in research. An effective strategy to becoming involved in a research project as an undergraduate involves the following steps:

- *Faculty research interests*: Find out the research interests of the faculty members in your psychology department. Your department may have a listing of faculty members and their research interests that you may view by going to the departmental Web site. If not, you may wish to schedule an appointment with individual faculty members to discuss their research.

- *Approaching a professor*: The next step involves asking a particular faculty member if he or she would consider having you as an undergraduate research assistant. Some faculty members may say yes or no right away. Others may ask you to work with them for a term on a trial basis to see if this work is something you really want to do or if you have the potential to become an active and contributing member of their research team.
- *Class participation*: Alternatively, you may take a course from a professor and find that you are interested in some of the same research areas as he or she is. Be sure to do well in the class by actively participating in class discussions and getting good scores on tests and quizzes. At the appropriate time, ask the professor if he or she would be willing to have you as a research assistant.

Note: Your research interests do not have to be exactly the same as the professor with whom you wish to work. However, there should be sufficient overlap so that you both will be happy with the assistantship. The important point is to obtain research experience.

Q32. How important are publications or conference presentations at the undergraduate level?

A32. Having a publication and/or a conference presentation documented in your application can be very impressive to admissions committees, depending upon the quality of the journal or conference. Having your name on a paper that is published in a respected psychological journal is a solid indication of your commitment to, and involvement in, scholarly research. The same goes for a presentation at a scholarly conference.

At a conference, you are more likely to present your work in the form of a poster at a poster session than to present your work orally in the form of a talk during a paper session (in which people deliver a 20-, 30-, or 60-minute talk) or symposium (in which a series of oral presentations are organized around closely related issues or topics). Poster sessions are generally 60- to 90-minute meetings in which people present their research in the form of a poster. Usually poster sessions are organized to cover similar or related topics. During the poster session, you stand by your poster and explain your work to interested people who stop by to read it or ask you specific questions about it. Poster presenters also customarily provide handouts describing their work.

An excellent outlet for undergraduate research in terms of conference presentations are the sessions at national meetings such as APA or APS and regional psychology conferences such as the Rocky Mountain Psychological Association or the Southeastern Psychological Association. In particular, all the conferences have undergraduate paper and poster sessions sponsored by Psi Chi (see http://www.psichi.org/conventions/ and http://www.apa.org/organizations/regionals.html for a listing and description of regional psychology conferences). Psi Chi created these sessions for the sole purpose of promoting undergraduate research presentations. In addition, some colleges and universities hold annual conferences that center exclusively on undergraduate research presentations.

Journals also exist as outlets for publishing undergraduate research. One popular undergraduate journal is the *Psi Chi journal of undergraduate research*. Information about the journal may be found online at http://www.psichi.org/pubs/journal/submissions.asp

Q33. What sorts of clinical experiences will strengthen my application to clinical psychology programs?

A33. Depending on the community in which you live, there may be many different options available to you to gain clinical experience: for example, group homes for the developmentally disabled; shelters for battered women, runaways, or the poverty stricken; summer camps for children and adolescents, including those for developmentally disabled persons; drug and alcohol rehabilitation centers; mental health centers and mental institutions; and college and university peer-counseling and tutoring programs. Most of these options will involve volunteer positions, although some may involve paid positions. Faculty members at your college or university should be able to provide you with specific information about the nature of the kind of programs that are available in your area. Many communities also publish "community resource directories" that list and describe organizations and agencies that provide volunteer opportunities.

Q34. Will becoming a member of Psi Chi (or other honorary societies, such as Psi Beta (the honor society for psychology students attending two-year colleges) help strengthen my application to graduate school?

A34. By itself, becoming a member of Psi Chi (or of other honorary societies or a student affiliate of APA or APS) will not greatly increase your chances of getting into graduate school. Although faculty view membership in Psi Chi favorably, they see it as being but one aspect of a well-rounded applicant. The purpose of becoming a member of Psi Chi is not to add another line to your vita or resume. Rather, its purpose is to become a member of a community that shares a common interest in psychology and that promotes greater understanding of the study of psychology. Psi Chi sponsors many useful and fun activities: for example, GRE study groups, regional and national research conferences, and undergraduate awards for research and scholarship. In addition, Psi Chi chapters usually have "libraries" full of graduate school bulletins from various schools as well as books and other information related to getting into graduate school.

In addition, many, if not most, applicants to graduate schools in psychology are Psi Chi members – thus, being a Psi Chi member doesn't distinguish you from other applicants. However, if you serve in a leadership role within your local Psi Chi chapter (president, vice-president, and so on), then you will stand out among the other applicants who have not assumed similar roles.

Keep in mind, too, that many psychology departments around the country also have psychology clubs for undergraduates. These clubs generally do not have the scholastic requirements for membership that Psi Chi does, but involvement with a psychology club, especially if you hold a leadership position, may give you valuable experience that will be looked upon favorably by members of admissions committees.

Q35. Will having a Master's degree before applying to doctoral programs help or hurt my chances of getting accepted at those programs?

A35. If you have done well in your Master's work (obtained a high GPA and satisfactorily completed a thesis) your chances of getting into a doctoral program may be a bit better than they might be otherwise. Remember, what is important is that once you start graduate study, do your best to produce high-quality work in the classroom, in research, and in any applied experiences you might undertake. It is your performance in these kinds of activities, and not merely possessing a Master's degree, that will impress admissions committees.

Q36. What is a vita? What kinds of activities should it describe?

A36. The word *vita* is Latin for "life." A vita is a resume or summary of your life's work. In this case, a vita is a summary of your life's work as it relates to your graduate school career. Preparing your vita will be useful for applying to graduate programs because it will contain all the information that a graduate program is likely to request of you. An outline for a vita and a sample vita are included in Appendix III.

Chapter 3
Choosing a Program: Navigating Your Way Through the Maze

One of the most important aspects of deciding to go to graduate school involves finding the graduate program that best meets your needs and abilities. You will need to know where to find the graduate programs that might be best suited to your career goals, how to distinguish good programs from mediocre ones, how much it will cost you to attend one program versus another program, and what kinds of financial aid different programs may have to offer. The questions and answers in this chapter are aimed at helping you select those graduate programs that may be best suited to your qualifications and interests. As you read through this chapter, you may find that Appendix II: General Concentrations of Psychology in Graduate School may be helpful in considering your options for selecting a specialty area and graduate program in psychology.

Q37. How can I find out which graduate programs best fit my interests and needs?

A37. The best source of information about which graduate programs may be most suitable to your interests and needs is the American Psychological Association's (APA's) *Graduate Study in Psychology*. This book describes every psychology graduate program in the United States and Canada. The book is organized alphabetically by state and by school. For each school, information is given concerning admissions criteria, the emphasis of the program, number of faculty, and average GPA and GRE scores. It also contains a useful index that is organized by type of program. This book may be ordered by writing, e-mailing, or calling APA at:

APA Service Center
750 First Street, NE
Washington, DC 20002-4242
Phone: 800-374-2721 or 202-336-5510
Fax: 202-335-5502
Monday through Friday, 9:00 a.m. to 6:00 p.m. Eastern Time.
e-mail: order@apa.org

The URL for APA Publications is http://www.apa.org/publications/

The URL for a description of *Graduate Study in Psychology* is http:// www.apa.org/books/4270088.html

Many bookstores keep this book in stock and others would be willing to order it for you. Check with your campus bookstore for further information.

In addition, there is a tremendous amount of information on the Internet about preparing for graduate study in psychology. However, because some Internet sites do not always contain the most recent information or even accurate information, you should be very careful about accepting all the information that these sites may tell you about graduate study in psychology. Certainly, though, some sites provide current and accurate information, but we will let you be the judge of that! One excellent way to start your Internet search is to select a search engine such as Google®, type in "Graduate Study in Psychology," click on the "go" button, and see where it takes you. Enjoy your search!

Q38. What should I look for in a good PhD program?

A38. Here are several key characteristics of a good PhD program:

- Program faculty work closely with their graduate students.
- Program faculty regularly publish in their field and make presentations at state, regional, national, and international conferences.
- The program is accredited or approved by appropriate organizations.
- The program emphasizes both high-quality research productivity and academic activity.
- Program faculty are tenured or tenure-track faculty.

- The department should be large enough that it has faculty who represent most or all of the major areas in modern psychology. The department should also be able to support or partially support, through assistantships and other means, graduate student study and research.
- Adequate facilities for research and practica.
- Much of this information is given in the APA's *Graduate Study in Psychology*. You can also learn more about specific graduate programs by e-mailing them directly, by calling and talking to faculty and graduate students who are members of that program, or by visiting that campus and learning first-hand the "lay of the land."

Q39. How do I select graduate programs that will be a "good fit" for me?

A39. There is no perfect way to know in advance which graduate programs are right for you. Your best bet is to find answers to the following questions:

- To what kind of career do you aspire?
- In what area of psychology are you the most strongly interested?
- What is your theoretical orientation (cognitive, behavioral, etc.)?

Once you have answers to these questions, you then must ask yourself one more question: Which graduate programs offer training consistent with my career aspirations, my professional interests, and my theoretical orientation? The best place to begin looking for answers to this question is the APA's *Graduate Study in Psychology*.

You may find that you save considerable time in your search for the right graduate program by also consulting with professors at your college or university and asking for their recommendations for suitable schools, given your background. You may also wish to visit or call faculty in programs that interest you to get a clearer picture of how those programs mesh with your goals. Another useful strategy is to use your online library resources after you have written away for admissions materials and search (using PsychLit or PsychInfo) for publications of key faculty to learn more about the work they have been doing in recent years.

Please keep in mind, though, that you need to be practical in making decisions about which graduate programs may be right for you. If your academic credentials are far below those required for acceptance into particular programs, you should not apply to them: Your time spent filling out applications and the money spent on application fees will be wasted. Apply to those graduate programs whose admission criteria you roughly meet or exceed.

Q40. If I am interested in working in a particular laboratory or with a particular person for my graduate work, do I contact him or her directly during the application process?

A40. The answer to this question is both yes and no. You should not contact particular laboratories or people for application materials. Instead, you should contact the specific psychology department with which the laboratory or person is affiliated. However, if you wish to request copies of research articles or express your interest in certain work, then you should feel free to make contact with particular persons. If you decide to write or e-mail someone about his or her work, though, make sure that your letter is thoughtful and well written (use correct grammar and make sure it is free of typographical errors). A letter that is over-complimentary of the professor's work, unfairly or naively critical of the professor's work, or is otherwise poorly prepared is likely to hurt you if you apply to the program with which that professor is affiliated. Be sure to do all your homework before you make personal contact with a professor or visit his or her campus. (The same advice is applicable to meeting professors at conferences – make sure you know what you are talking about before you engage them in a discussion of their research.)

Note: In some graduate programs, you are accepted into the program; in others, you are accepted to work with a specific faculty member (you'll be notified which of these alternatives is true for you in the acceptance letter you receive from the graduate program). In the first case, you have the freedom to work on different projects with different faculty. In the second case, it is assumed that you will be working exclusively with one faculty member.

Q41. What does it mean for a clinical or counseling graduate program to be "APA accredited"?

A41. To be "APA accredited" means that a particular program has met the minimum standards for clinical and counseling training established by the American Psychological Association. Among the requirements are criteria relating to faculty credentials, coursework, licensure, research and clinical opportunities, and internships for clinical and counseling students. If you are working in an APA-accredited clinical or counseling program, you will be more likely to be successful in competing for internships than if you are working in a clinical or counseling program that is not APA accredited. Other organizations besides APA may accredit other kinds of programs. You may wish to check into accreditation further by contacting those graduate programs in which you are interested.

Q42. To how many graduate programs should I apply? Should I apply to more programs than just my top choices?

A42. You should definitely apply to more programs than your top one or two choices. It is always a good idea to have several backup options. To how many programs you should apply will be determined by your own personal situation, but a rough rule is to apply to 8 to 12 graduate programs. Several of these programs should be your top choices; the remainder should be those whose admission requirements you know you roughly meet or exceed. One strategy for determining to which programs you should apply is called the "strategy of thirds." One-third of the programs to which you apply should be exceptional graduate programs whose admission criteria are very stringent, but are roughly compatible with your credentials, one-third should be very good graduate programs, whose admission criteria are equivalent to or less than your credentials, and one-third should be to graduate programs whose admission criteria you can easily meet.

Keep in mind that each program will require that you send in an "application fee" with your application. These fees can be expensive and add up quickly, depending on the number of schools to which you apply (see Q & A 59). However, a wise perspective to take on the cost of applying to graduate school is that it is truly an investment in your future, which could pay off handsomely for you over the long run in terms of the employment opportunities that will come your way with an advanced degree relative to a Bachelor's degree.

Q43. How much is it going to cost me to go to graduate school?

A43. The cost of graduate education varies tremendously depending upon which school you decide to attend. Tuition costs and estimates of living costs are usually given in the packet of information you will receive in response to your request for application materials. Tuition costs for individual schools are also given in the APA's *Graduate Study in*

Psychology. Tuition, fees, and books may cost as little as $2,000 a year at some graduate schools and as high as $30,000 or more a year at others. Many graduate schools extend tuition waivers or remissions to students, so students only pay for books, which can cost several hundred dollars or more per academic term. Other graduate schools require that all students, including out-of-state students, pay only in-state tuition. Many graduate schools also provide graduate teaching and research assistantships to the students they have accepted.

Q44. What is involved in a graduate assistantship?

A44. A graduate assistantship involves performing a service, usually by assisting a faculty member teach an undergraduate course or conducting research for a particular faculty member, in return for a stipend. These assistantships are often limited in number and therefore may be competitive. Graduate teaching assistantships may involve assisting in the teaching of a course, such as grading papers and tests, teaching a laboratory section of a course, occasionally giving lectures and demonstrations to undergraduate students, or actually assuming responsibility for the teaching of a course. Graduate research assistantships generally involve assuming the responsibility for carrying out a major portion of a study, including running subjects, overseeing day-to-day activities involved in carrying out a study, analyzing and graphing data, and helping prepare written research reports for presentation or publication (or both).

In some cases, assistantships may not available within the psychology department to which you have applied or been accepted. However, at many institutions, assistantships are often available outside the department. For example, campus teaching and learning centers – which focus on graduate student and faculty development – sometimes will hire graduate student assistants to help run various programs (workshops and other presentations) they sponsor.

Q45. How do I get a graduate assistantship?

A45. Assistantships are generally a part of the offer you receive when you are notified that you have been accepted into a particular program. At some schools, all first-year graduate students receive the same type of assistantship. The specific duties to be performed under the assistantship generally focus on either teaching (Graduate Teaching Assistant) or research (Graduate Research Assistant). Usually the assistantship is limited to a specific number of years of support. If you don't finish the program requirements within this time period, you may have to find an alternative source of income to help you complete your studies.

Q46. How important is it that professors at the schools I apply to have the same research interests as I do?

A46. Very important. If you wish to learn and master a particular area within psychology it only makes sense that you seek training from experts in those areas. Graduate professors are especially interested in training graduate students who share their research and scholarly interests. If your interests are not well formed when the time comes to apply to graduate programs, you may wish to apply to a general Master's program prior to PhD programs. Doing so will give you some time to form solid interests while also earning academic credit toward your degree.

Chapter 4
The GRE: *The* Test

The Graduate Record Examination or GRE is a standardized test that most graduate programs in psychology require you take as a means of providing additional information about your intellectual potential. The thought of taking the GRE has struck fear into the heart of many undergraduates simply because so many graduate programs rely heavily on the information it provides for judging the quality of their applications. The questions and answers in this chapter are aimed at providing you with a clear picture of what the GRE is, how your scores on it are used to determine the viability of your application, when it should be taken, how much it costs to take, how to prepare for it, and whether you should take it more than once.

Q47. What is the GRE?

A47. The GRE is an aptitude test developed by ETS (Educational Testing Service: www.gre.org or www.ets.org/gre) and is used to assess your academic knowledge and intellectual skills relevant to success in graduate school. The purpose of the GRE is to provide graduate programs with a quantitative assessment or estimate of an applicant's potential to do well in graduate school in a format that can be compared easily to estimates of other applicants. An excellent overview of the GRE, including information for registering for it, may be found at http://ftp.ets.org/pub/gre/727122.pdf

The GRE includes the General Test and the Subject Test. The General Test assesses your critical thinking abilities, analytical writing skills, verbal reasoning abilities, and quantitative reasoning skills. The General Test yields three scores: analytical, verbal, and quantitative, although many, if not most, schools use only the verbal and quantitative scores in determining your aptitude for their graduate programs.

The Subject Test examines your particular specialty area, in this case, psychology. Most graduate programs require that applicants take only the General Test. The Psychology Subject Test yields three scores: one for experimental psychology, one for social psychology, and a total score.

The GRE is available in a computerized version and in a paper-and-pencil version, although the paper-and-pencil version is only offered in those areas in which the computerized version is not available. (However, as of this writing the Subject Test is offered only in a paper-and-pencil format.) GRE computer-based centers are located throughout the United States, Canada, and many other countries throughout the world. To locate a GRE computer-based test center near you, go to: http://www.etsis4.ets.org/tcenter/

You may register for the GRE online at http://www.ets.org/gre or by calling 800-GRE-CALL (473-2255). You may also register by mail by obtaining a registration form from ETS and returning it to them. The fastest way to register is online or by phone. Please note that ETS is currently planning to introduce a revised version of the General Test in October 2006. Among other things, this test has been revised to enhance its validity, increase security measures, and provide college and universities with improved information about test-takers' performance.

Q48. Do all schools require both the GRE General Test and the Subject Test?

A48. No, but at least some of the graduate programs to which you apply will request that you provide scores for both tests. You may wish to take them both when you have the chance, rather than taking the General Test at one time and the Subject Test at a later time. However, the GRE tests can be a grueling experience, and you may find that taking both of the tests closely in time can be overwhelming. If you suspect that this problem might be the case for you, then schedule to take the GRE tests at two different times – one day for General Test and another day for the Subject Test.

Information regarding a graduate program's minimal acceptable GRE scores is usually stated in a form that combines scores from the verbal and quantitative subtests (called the "composite score"), for example, "The minimum GRE score required is 1200." However, you should be aware that some graduate programs look at the individual verbal and quantitative subscores that are summed to yield the composite score. Knowing the individual subscores tips the admissions committee to your relative strengths in these two areas. Thus, your overall score may be high, say a 1240, but there may be a large difference in your subtest scores, say, 480 on your verbal subtest and 760 on your quantitative subtest. The low verbal subtest score may be interpreted by an admissions committee as your having a weakness in this area, which could hurt your chances of acceptance.

Q49. Are GRE scores the most important part of the application materials?

A49. Remember, your GRE score is assumed to reflect your general intellectual ability and your potential for success in graduate school. The GRE cannot assess all the skills that may determine your acceptance into a graduate program. Other factors such as GPA, research experience, and letters of recommendation also are important in an admissions committee's decision to accept or reject an applicant. What is important to remember is that some admissions committees weigh GRE scores more heavily than others in assessing an applicant's qualifications.

Many graduate schools typically use a formula that differentially weighs quantitative factors such as GRE scores and GPA. Different graduate schools assign different weights or importance to these factors. The higher the score derived from the formula, the better the applicant's chances of being accepted. In fact, most graduate schools have established firm cut-off points based on the use of the formula. If an applicant's formula-derived score falls below this cut-off point, the applicant is no longer considered for admission to that program. Applicants whose scores equal or exceed the cut-off point move on to the next step of the admissions process. Although GRE is only one element that figures into the formula, it is an important part: Obtaining the highest GRE score possible is essential to moving on to the next step of the admissions process.

The formula is actually used as a screening device: Admissions committees often don't even begin to look closely at a person's application unless that person has a formula-derived score equaling or exceeding the cut-off point. The formula, then, saves admissions committees an enormous amount of time in evaluating applicants' credentials for their graduate program.

Q50. When should the GRE be taken?

A50. You should take the GRE in the spring of your junior year so that your scores can be sent to the graduate programs to which you are applying by the application deadline, which is usually sometime in late January or early February of the following year. To allow sufficient time to retake the GRE, should you be dissatisfied with your scores, you should register to take the GRE no later than in the summer of your junior year. At the absolute very latest, you should take or retake the GRE in October of your senior year.

The General Test may be taken year round in the United States and Canada. However, you should be aware that the General Test may be only taken once within any calendar month and that it cannot be taken more than five times within any single one-year period.

Q51. How good do my GRE scores have to be in order to get accepted into graduate school?

A51. Acceptance criteria for graduate school vary from graduate program to graduate program. However, minimum GRE scores for prestigious graduate programs generally fall in the 1200 to 1400 range. Master's degree programs often have lower GRE requirements.

For specific score requirements established for the schools to which you may be applying, consult the APA's *Graduate Study in Psychology*, which lists each graduate program's minimum score for acceptance, a preferred score for acceptance, and the average score for the students who entered that program the previous year. Also, consult specific graduate program's application materials for their particular minimum score requirements.

Q52. Can the GRE be taken more than once? What are the chances of obtaining a better score if I retake the GRE?

A52. You can take the GRE as many times as you are willing to pay for it (as of this writing, $115 for the General Test and $130 for the Subject Test). Taking the GRE more than once can improve your scores (through practice effects), although not necessarily by a large margin. According to the ETS (http://www.ets.org/Media/Tests/GRE/pdf/994994.pdf), the average gain in score is about 20–30 points on the General and Subject Tests. ETS will report all GRE scores taken within any five-year window of time to the schools to which you are applying. Remember, you may take the GRE once per month, but no more than five times in any given year.

However, retaking the GRE can have its drawbacks. Some schools will average all of your GRE scores over the last five years. You should also pay attention to your score in relation to the national average GRE score. If you scored well the first time (perhaps a score of 1200 or greater) and you take the test again, you may to do poorer on the retake due to statistical regression. However, if you pay close attention to the questions that were difficult for you, and study these areas intently, you may improve your scores. Remember, all of your scores from previous administrations within the past five years will be reported to the schools to which you request they be sent.

Q53. How do I send my GRE scores to the schools to which I am applying?

A53. ETS will automatically send your scores to four graduate schools and/or fellowships of your choice. Your scores will be reported 10 to 15 days after you take the test. The price for this service is included in your registration fee. Additional reports of your scores may be sent at a cost of $15 per report up to five years after you have taken the GRE.

You will find that on your registration form there is a space to list the codes of schools to which you desire your scores to be sent. The school codes are listed in the *GRE Bulletin* that you will find in your registration packet.

Remember, if you take the GRE more than once you should be aware that cumulative reporting takes place. This means that all the scores for the last five years will be reported to the schools you have chosen. Some graduate programs will average all the reported scores for the last five years and others will use only the most recent scores.

Q54. How should I prepare for taking the GRE?

A54. First, you should obtain the *GRE Information and Registration Bulletin.* Included in this publication is information regarding the different types of questions on the tests, test dates, scoring of the tests, registering for the GRE tests, ordering preparation materials, and reporting of your scores to schools. You should become thoroughly familiar with all the information in this publication prior to taking the GRE, especially how the tests are administered and scored.

The bulletin is free and may be obtained via the Internet or by land mail. To access the Internet version, go to www.gre.org and scroll down a short way and under "Test-takers" click on "Get Information and Registration Bulletin." From there follow the directions. Instructions for obtaining a mailed copy of the Information and Registration

Bulletin are also given on this page. Again, just follow the directions provided.

Second, you should become thoroughly familiar with the GRE itself. You should begin studying for the GRE at least three months prior to the examination date. If you feel weak in either the verbal or quantitative areas or both, you should develop study strategies to improve your chances of obtaining the best possible score.

You should obtain the GRE Practice Book for the General Test (10th edition), which is available on the ETS Web site for $21 (http://www.gre.org; locate "Resources for Test-takers" in the menu bar on the left side of the page and then follow the directions for locating the information about the Practice Book).

This book contains seven previously administered versions of the paper-and-pencil GRE General Test. One of the versions includes detailed explanations of the questions and answers. It also contains a wealth of other information regarding how to prepare for the GRE General Test.

Another effective strategy, although it costs more, is to take a GRE preparation course from professional tutoring schools, such as the the Stanley H. Kaplan Educational Center Ltd., and the Princeton Review. There is a cost for these "prep" course and it can be very expensive. These courses are offered throughout the country. For further information about such courses contact:

Kaplan Educational Center Ltd.
http://www.kaptest.com
800-KAP-TEST

Princeton Review
http://www.princetonreview.com/home.asp
800-333-0369

Number 2 (online only)
http://number2.com

If you do not have the money to spend on these kinds of courses, brush up on your algebra, geometry, and verbal skills by reviewing and studying your notes from classes you may have taken in the past. You may wish to consider taking a math class the term before you take the GRE.

If you are taking the Psychology Subject Test you should review the materials you have kept from your psychology courses. Roughly 40 percent of the questions on this test cover topics such as "learning, language, memory, thinking, sensation and perception, physiological psychology, ethology, and comparative psychology." Your answers to these questions are figured into both your subscore for experimental psychology and your total score for the test. Another 43 percent of the test is derived from the following areas: "clinical and abnormal, developmental, personality, and social psychology." Your answers to these questions are figured into both your subscore for social psychology and your total score for the test. Finally, the remaining questions cover "history of psychology, applied psychology, measurement, research designs, and statistics." Your answers to these questions are figured into your total score for the test.*

If you have not kept your course materials, you should obtain an introductory psychology text and study it thoroughly. Faculty in your psychology department should be able to provide you with a good recommendation as to which introductory texts are most suitable for studying for the GRE. Also check with your local Psi Chi chapter for additional resources and information.

Remember, GRE scores play an integral part of an admissions committee's decision to admit applicants into their programs. Obtain the very best possible score that you can.

*This information was taken directly from the GRE Web site (http://www.ets.org)

Chapter 5
The Application Process:
Doing the Paperwork

The nuts and bolts of applying to graduate school, the what-to-dos and the what-not-to-dos, can be complicated and frustrating. The questions and answers in this chapter center on the specifics involved in putting together your application to graduate school. When you finish reading this chapter you will know how to obtain graduate school applications, what additional materials should accompany your application, how to write an effective letter of intent, how to obtain favorable letters of recommendation, when applications are to be submitted, to how many graduate schools you should consider applying, and how admissions committees are likely to evaluate your application materials.

Q55. How do I obtain applications for graduate school?

A55. Before obtaining applications, you first need to identify which types of psychology programs you are interested in and then find out which schools offer programs in those areas. Additionally, the APA publishes *Graduate Study in Psychology*, which describes every psychology graduate program in the United States and Canada. Each program's admission and degree requirements are listed along with their Web sites, mailing addresses, phone numbers, and demographic data on their students. This book may be ordered by writing, e-mailing, or calling APA at:

APA Service Center
750 First Street, NE
Washington, DC 20002-4242
Phone: 800-374-2721 or 202-336-5510
Fax: 202-335-5502

Monday through Friday, 9:00 a.m. to 6:00 p.m. Eastern Time.
e-mail: order@apa.org

The URL for APA Publications is http://www.apa.org/publications/

The URL for a description of *Graduate Study in Psychology* is http://
www.apa.org/books/4270088.html

Once you have identified the programs of interest to you, write (either
through e-mail or US Post) to those programs, all of which are located
within departments of psychology, requesting that they send you admissions information. (Note that many schools will have all their admission
information online, including their application forms.) This information
will include descriptions of the program, admissions requirements, course
requirements, financial aid information, assistantships, and an application form or packet.

Because many graduate schools send out their application materials
in bulk mail, the materials may be delayed in reaching you. Expect
at least a two- or three-week delay between the time you request
applications materials and the actual time you receive them. Therefore,
using an online application has an advantage in that you are not waiting
for an application to arrive through land mail.

Q56. Can I apply for admission during any term, or are there only
certain terms in which I can be admitted?

A56. Some graduate schools, especially those with only Master's degree programs have open admission dates, which means that you may be able to
start at the beginning of any term. However, most doctoral programs
and many Master's degree programs admit students only in the fall
term, which means that these programs have December 1 to February 1
application deadlines. To know which schools have open dates and
which do not, consult APA's *Graduate Study in Psychology* and check
with the departments to which you are applying by looking at their
Web sites or telephoning them.

Note: Some graduate schools accept or reject students as their applications
arrive, so do not delay in getting your application materials in the mail. They
often do not wait for the deadline or do not wait until applications are completed. In some cases, graduate schools have filled their available slots for new
graduate students before the deadlines they posted for receipt of materials!

Q57. What is included in my application materials that I will be submitting to graduate programs?

A57. In general, your application materials will include the following items:

- Your completed application form (which can often be completed online).
- A copy of your undergraduate and/or Master's transcript.
- Your GRE scores.
- If you speak English as a second language you will need to submit your TOEFL scores.
- A letter of intent (sometimes called the "personal statement").
- At least three letters of recommendation. (These are often mailed separately by your letter writers.)
- Reprints of published papers or preprints of any papers that have been submitted for publication on which you are an author.

Some programs may not request that you submit *all* of these items. Some programs will only ask for *some* of these items. Only send in those items that are specifically requested by the program to which you are applying. Most schools will not ask you to send in your vita – the purpose of preparing your vita is to organize relevant personal and professional information to help you complete application materials.

Note: Be sure to *type* your application and all materials that you submit with it. It is not unheard of for admissions committees to reject an otherwise solid application simply because it was submitted in handwritten form.

Q58. What weight do admissions committees give each component of the application?

A58. Most admissions committees will give more weight to the quantitative aspects of your application than to other aspects, which means that the most important components of your application are your GRE scores and GPA. After that, admissions committees look to letters of recommendation, research experience, and letters of intent to help them decide who among the pool of applicants shows the most promise of becoming a high-caliber graduate student. (Research experience will likely be documented by persons who write your letters of recommendation and you should describe it in your letter of intent.)

Note: In an article published in *Teaching of Psychology*, Drew Appleby and Karen Appleby described five "kisses of death" in the graduate school application process. Their article is based on a survey of 88 chairs of graduate admissions committees across the US. The kisses of death are: (a) weak letters of intent (personal statements), (b) weak letters of recommendation, (c) poor writing skills on the part of the applicant, (d) inappropriate attempts to impress the admissions committee, and (e) lack of the applicant's knowledge of the graduate program to which he or she is applying.

The complete reference for this article is:

Appleby, D. C., & Appleby, K. M. (2006). Kisses of death in the graduate school application process. *Teaching of Psychology, 33*, 19–24.

Q59. How much does it cost to apply to graduate school?

A59. Most graduate schools charge application fees in the range of $25 to $50. However, other schools may have slightly higher application fees. The application fee is typically posted on the Web site of the school to which you are applying. If you plan on applying to 10 schools, you will likely spend at least $300. When you add this amount to the cost of photocopying materials, transcript fees, GRE mailing fees, envelopes, and postage, your expenses may run as high as $500. If you live on a tight budget already, you'll need to start saving during your sophomore or junior years to be able to pay for these expenses. Also, be mindful that there will be financial costs involved when you go on your campus visits and interviews.

Q60. If materials, such as my GRE scores or transcripts, are sent to graduate schools before I apply to those schools, what will happen to them?

A60. Arrival of GRE scores, transcripts, and letters of recommendation before the arrival of the actual application at graduate schools is very common and is nothing about which you should be concerned. These materials are simply held until the application arrives. At that time, the application and materials that arrived early are placed together in the same folder.

Q61. What will happen to my application if some of the application materials arrive after the deadline?

A61. The answer to this question depends on the graduate program. Some schools will not review applications that arrive after the deadline; other programs will. Your best bet is to start the application process early in the fall term to insure that all your application materials arrive before the deadline.

It is a good idea to check with each graduate program to which you have applied well before the application deadline to determine which of your application materials have arrived. If any materials are missing, you will still have ample time to get them in.

Q62. What will make my application stand out from the others?

A62. Assuming that you have competitive GRE scores (1200 plus), a high cumulative GPA (3.5 or above), and a clearly written letter of intent (make sure your letter of intent refers to that particular school to which you are applying), two aspects of your application become very important: (a) your description of your research experience and (b) your letters of recommendation. If your letters of recommendation are very strong, meaning that they speak to your developing analytical and professional qualities, and you have participated as an undergraduate research assistant (played an active, ongoing role in helping a professor or two conduct their research), your application will catch the eye of the admissions committee. It is important to keep in mind that one of the best ways to secure good letters of recommendation is to serve as an undergraduate research assistant. Through this experience faculty members will get to know many important aspects about you (e.g., your work ethic, your ability to be reliable and responsible) and can write letters of recommendation containing solid information regarding your potential as a graduate student.

Another tack you may take, which also assumes that you have a competitive application, is to mention in your letter of intent the faculty person with whom you wish to work. If you do so, be sure to spell out, in clear terms, the reasons why you would like to work with this particular faculty member. Specifically, one important reason that you should mention is that you have the same interests as this person and that you know of his or her reputation in these areas. (Letter 3 in Appendix IV is a good example of how to express this issue.)

Q63. What is a letter of intent? What should I write in my letter of intent?

A63. A letter of intent is a brief statement of your educational goals and career aspirations, a description of your academic credentials, and your rationale for pursuing graduate education. The letter of intent should be brief (usually one to two pages), typed (single-spaced), neat, and to the point. Review it carefully for typographical and grammatical errors before including it among your application materials.

Important: A letter of intent containing typos and grammatical errors will create an unfavorable impression of your potential for graduate work. Be professional. Although the letter may be organized in various ways, it should contain the following information:

- A direct statement of your educational goals and career aspirations.
- A brief account of your interests in particular areas of psychology and how they developed.
- A short description of your academic history with special attention to any specific skills you may have acquired during your under-graduate career (e.g., computer or other technical skills, math or statistical skills, related work, research, teaching, or clinical skills).
- A brief account of how your educational or work-related experiences have specifically shaped your desire to go to graduate school.
- The specific reasons why you have selected that particular school as a potential program for your graduate training.
- The letter of intent is your opportunity to call attention to strengths that might not be readily apparent in your other application materials. Try to keep the letter of intent professional; avoid lengthy in-depth personal histories involving friends and family members. Also avoid statements such as "I want to become a psychologist because I want to help people," "People have always told me that I am a good listener and that I am easy to talk to," or "People always seem to come to me with their problems." These kinds of statements could apply to almost anybody and do not serve as relevant qualifications to do graduate work in psychology.

Your description of your educational and career goals should be well defined, although not so narrow or specific as to give faculty the impression that you are not an open-minded individual whose intellectual development during graduate school is unlikely to be influenced by their teaching and mentoring. Appendix IV contains three sample letters of intent.

Q64. Should I write the same letter of intent to all the programs to which I am applying, sort of a form letter, or should I tailor my letter to each of them?

A64. Although tailoring your letter to each graduate program to which you apply is time consuming, you will increase your chances of favorably impressing each of the different admissions committees by doing so. A letter tailored to a specific program is more likely to reveal to the admissions committee that you have, in fact, done your homework in researching that program's emphasis and faculty interests. The core of your letter of intent, which describes your experiences, interests, and aspirations could be the same or similar for each of your letters – but by carefully adding a sentence here and there that directly relates this information to a specific program, your letter will come across as being more articulate and thoughtful. (Letter 3 in Appendix IV is a good example of this technique.)

Q65. How many letters of recommendation will I need?

A65. Most graduate programs require that applications be accompanied by at least three letters of recommendation. Be sure you follow each graduate school's request for the specific number of letters of recommendation that you need. Sending more letters of recommendation than the program requires may not help your application in any way.

About two weeks before the application deadline, you should contact (typically a phone call or an e-mail will suffice) each of the graduate schools to which you have applied and inquire if all of your letters of recommendation have been received. If not, ask which letters have been received. You then should immediately contact the professor or professors who have not submitted a letter for you and gently remind them to send their letters in – two weeks still gives them ample time to write the letter and submit it.

Q66. Who should I select to write my letters of recommendation? What sorts of things should I expect my writers of letters of recommendation to say about me?

A66. Your letters of recommendation should be written by faculty members who know you well. Preferably, your letters should be written by faculty who can speak to your work habits, your writing and speaking skills, and your personal characteristics such as dependability, self-motivation, ability to assume responsibility, intelligence, ability to work well with others, your aptitude for research, and leadership potential. Faculty who know you only as a student in class will be in a less favorable position to write you a thorough letter of recommendation than faculty with whom you have worked as an undergraduate research assistant.

Q67. What makes for a strong letter of recommendation?

A67. Your strongest letters of recommendation are most likely to be written by professors who know you well outside of the classroom (e.g. your Psi Chi advisor or those faculty for whom you have served as an undergraduate research assistant or an undergraduate teaching assistant.) If your letters are written by only professors who know you as a student who has taken a course or two from them, all they can do is to describe your class work. This kind of information can be easily inferred from your transcript, so the letter is not adding any information not already available in other parts of your application.

In addition, even if your letter writers describe you as an "A" student, their letters are not very useful to the admissions committee. The vast majority of students applying to graduate school have "As" in their courses, too.

What admissions committees really want letters of recommendation to do is to distinguish the applicants in some noteworthy way. Letters that describe your willingness and ability to accept responsibility, ability to grasp difficult concepts and ideas, devotion to research or to a particular area, ability to work with others, your "teachability" in non-classroom settings, your initiative, and your ambitions are the best kind of letters.

Letters describing these sorts of characteristics are not usually written by professors who know you only as a student. Having professors who know you in only this capacity often suggests to admissions committees that you are not really committed enough to psychology to go beyond classroom work, that you decided late in your undergraduate career to seek graduate training, or that you haven't taken the time to develop your career interests enough to get better letters of recommendation. Uninformative or poor letters of recommendation can hurt your chances of being accepted into graduate school; strong letters can help make your application more competitive.

Q68. Do all my letter writers have to be written by psychologists?

A68. Not all your letter writers need to be psychologists, although at least two of them should be; one could be a faculty member in a different department. If all your letter writers are not psychologists, they should at least be people who are qualified to assess your work habits, intelligence, judgment, integrity, and other characteristics related to your potential to do well in graduate school. A work supervisor, preferably in a psychology-related field, would be satisfactory. Persons with whom you have strictly a personal relationship are not usually able to provide admissions committees with the kind of information needed to render a favorable judgment of your application materials.

Q69. How do I get to know my professors better so I can ask them to write letters of recommendation for me?

A69. The best way to get to know your professors better, in terms of positioning yourself to ask them to write letters of recommendation, is to volunteer to work with them as an undergraduate research assistant or to take an independent study or readings course from them. Only by working closely with you on outside-of-the-classroom projects can faculty gain an accurate picture of the kind of graduate student you may become. A letter of recommendation is a professional assessment of your potential to complete graduate work successfully.

Q70. Should I provide my letter writers with any additional information about me, such as my academic record or my goals for graduate school?

A70. Although the faculty whom you plan to ask to write your letters of recommendation may know your capabilities as a research assistant and student, they may not have access to information that may help them write you a complete letter of recommendation. At the time you request a faculty member to write you a letter of recommendation, you should give him or her a copy of your vita, which describes your academic history, academic goals, and career aspirations (see the outline for the vita and sample vita in Appendix III). Your vita will provide your letter writers with your complete background as a potential graduate student, which may help them paint a clearer, more favorable picture of your skills and talents in their letters. On some occasions, a letter writer may consult other faculty or even Graduate Teaching Assistants (GTAs) who have had you in class so as to get a better picture of the kind of person you are and the type of graduate student you are likely to become.

Q71. How much time should I give my professors to write my letters of recommendation?

A71. Generally speaking, you should give your letter writers between four and six weeks to write your letters. That means that you must be aware of the application deadlines for each of the schools to which you are applying. When you give your letter writers your vita, also give them a list of schools to which you are applying. Next to the name of each school, you should note, in bold-faced, capitalized, and underlined print, the corresponding *APPLICATION DEADLINE*.

A *reiteration*: About two weeks before the application deadline, you should contact each of the graduate schools to which you have applied and inquire if all of your letters of recommendation have been received. If not, ask which letters they have received. You then should immediately contact the professor or professors who have not submitted a letter for you – two weeks still gives them ample time to write the letter and submit it before the deadline.

Chapter 6
The Interview:
How to Make the
Right Impression

If your application is competitive with those of other persons applying to the same graduate program, you are likely to be invited to an
on-campus interview hosted by the faculty in that program. The interview is used to help faculty members make the final decision regarding
which of the top applicants to accept into their program. The interview,
then, can make or break you, so to speak. The questions and answers in
this chapter concern the specifics of the interview, including scheduling,
what kinds of questions you might be asked, how you should dress, and
how to behave. In general, the aim of this chapter is two-fold. First, to
fill you in on the details of the interview, and, second, to make you
feel more at ease with the prospect of meeting admissions committee
members and other graduate program faculty face-to-face (or in talking
to them over the phone, in the case of a phone interview).

Q72. What is the purpose of the interview? How important is the
interview for being accepted to graduate school?

A72. Not all graduate programs schedule face-to-face interviews. Many either
don't hold an interview or interview their higher ranked applicants over
the phone. For those graduate programs that do hold interviews, the
purpose of the interview is three-fold. First, it is for graduate faculty to
meet you face-to-face to learn more about how well your interests,
skills, and abilities match those of their program. Second, the faculty
are interested in assessing your poise and professionalism. Third, it is
for you to learn how well you may fit into the program in terms of
faculty interests, interactions with other graduate students, how well

you like the general intellectual and social climate of the school, and the characteristics of the city or town in which the school is located. These objectives of the interview hold true regardless of the type of graduate program to which you might apply (e.g., clinical, experimental, social).

Doing well in your interview is critical to your acceptance to a graduate program. Being invited for an interview means that you are in the top tier of applicants being considered by the graduate faculty. In essence, the interview is a golden opportunity for you to impress the faculty with both your personal and professional qualities, and thereby increase your chances of being accepted into their graduate program. Not interviewing or doing poorly during the interview may put you at a distinct disadvantage relative to the other applicants being interviewed.

Q73. How is the interview scheduled?

A73. To conserve time and effort, many graduate programs schedule a single campus visitation day so that all applicants can be interviewed on the same day. The itinerary for the day is set by the faculty and usually includes individual interviews with graduate faculty, a lunch with faculty and graduate students, a tour of the department and laboratory facilities, a college or university dinner, and a party with the graduate students. In a situation where you cannot be on campus on the visitation day, you should inquire whether it would be possible for you to visit on an alternative day. However, if at all possible, try to arrange your schedule so that you can make the visitation day.

Phone interviews are usually scheduled in advance by a graduate faculty member. He or she will call you to arrange a mutually agreeable time for a conference call.

Q74. What is the difference between a phone interview and a face-to-face interview?

A74. A phone interview is usually a conference call in which two or more graduate faculty ask the applicant questions. At many schools, the phone interview is a preliminary interview used to screen applicants for the face-to-face interview. At other schools, the phone interview is the only interview there is. During the phone interview, you should conduct yourself professionally and show the interviewers respect and courtesy – just as you would during a face-to-face interview. (For example, unless you are told otherwise, address each faculty member by his or her title rather than his or her first name.) Another important difference between the two interviews is that the applicant is unable to visit campus and learn first-hand the nature of the school, the graduate program, the faculty, and the graduate students. Keep in mind, nothing can fully replace the in-person interview. If at all possible, when campus interviews are being held and you have been invited, choose to visit the graduate program for an interview. The phone interview will give you much needed information, but you will learn more about your future program if you interview in person, and they will learn more about you.

Q75. How should I prepare for the interview?

A75. In a sense, your entire undergraduate career has prepared you for the interview. Many of the questions you will be asked will concern your academic history and the future for which it has prepared you. However, you must still do some homework, especially with regard to the graduate program for which you are interviewing. In particular, make sure you are familiar with faculty research and teaching interests, program requirements, and something about the school and city or town in which the school is located. This information should be contained in the materials sent to you by the psychology department when you initially requested application materials. Prepare questions in advance that you would like to ask the faculty and the graduate students during your interview.

You may find it useful to practice for the interview: Ask a faculty member at your school to ask you questions typical of the interview you might experience in the weeks ahead.

Q76. Will contacting professors at the schools to which I have applied increase my chances of getting an interview?

A76. Contacting the psychology department to check on the status of your application (whether it is complete or not) is fine, but you should not establish contact in an attempt to persuade or convince faculty members to review your application favorably. Contacting faculty, especially if you do so repeatedly, may be viewed as an annoyance and as being unprofessional. Remember that, more than anything else, faculty are looking for graduate students who are not only bright, but who will represent their graduate program and their discipline in a professional style. Nonetheless, you should not hesitate to contact specific faculty members for professional reasons, such as learning more about their research program.

Q77. How should I dress for the interview?

A77. You should dress conservatively – remember, this is your only chance to make a favorable person-to-person impression on those faculty who will be evaluating your application. Men should wear slacks, jacket, dress shirt, and tie. Women should wear a dress, skirt and top/sweater, or slacks and top/sweater. In many cases, a party with graduate students and faculty occurs during the interview visit. For these, you may dress more casually. During the visit to campus, you will receive a tour of the grounds and often visit the library. Wear comfortable shoes for walking.

Q78. How should I behave during the interview?

A78. At all times during the interview you should behave professionally – treat everyone you meet with respect and courtesy. Here are some tips for how to behave during the interview:

- Ask relevant questions respectfully. Be specific with these questions. The more concrete you are about questions pertaining to a particular graduate program, the more the faculty will take into consideration that you are serious about their specific program.
- Meet as many faculty and graduate students as you can. Feel free to inquire about their specific interests and work.
- Be confident.
- Be positive and enthusiastic. Let the faculty know that you are very pleased to be interviewing with them.
- Emphasize what you know and what your interests are, not who you know. "Name dropping" in an interview is often not helpful.
- Offer a firm handshake when greeting faculty and graduate students, but otherwise do not touch faculty members, graduate students, or other applicants. Do not flirt under any circumstances.
- Alcohol may be offered with dinner. Drink in extreme moderation. Kindly refuse alcohol if you don't drink.
- Always use appropriate language, do not use profanity.
- Initiate topics of conversation about which you are knowledgeable. Stay away from discussing issues about which you know little or nothing.
- It is appropriate to say "I don't know" to questions to which you don't know the answer. Do not try to bluff your way through an answer.
- Engage in lively discussion with the interviewers; however, it isn't wise to argue for or against particular theoretical positions. Although

you may find faculty who hold the same views that you do, you are also likely to find other faculty who do not. There is no need to turn these faculty off to you and your application. In addition, faculty are likely to know more about the theory than you do, which can hurt you if they decide to plumb the depths of your knowledge.

- Allow the faculty and students to learn a little about you. However, do not regale the faculty, graduate students, and other applicants with your whole life story.
- Be confident in giving direct, to-the-point answers. Speak with enthusiasm, sincerity, and candor. Do not be flippant.
- Make eye contact with faculty – do not look down or away from faculty when answering their questions or when you pose questions to them.
- Be confident about what you have already accomplished without bragging about past successes. Your job during the interview is not to show the graduate faculty that you are better than the other applicants they are interviewing. Instead, it is to present yourself as a person of high academic and personal standards who knows what it means to act and speak professionally.

Q79. What kinds of questions will I be asked in the interview?

A79. The kinds of questions you will be asked during your interview will vary from program to program and from department to department. In general, though, you are likely to respond to questions along the following lines:

- With which professors would you most like to study?
- Why do you want to study psychology at this school in this particular program?
- What are your personal assets as far as being a good student and a potential professional in the field of psychology?
- What is your academic background and which particular courses have had the greatest influence on you? Make sure to mention courses outside of psychology – faculty enjoy engaging with well-rounded students.
- What are your specific interests in attending this graduate program?
- What are your specific interests within psychology and what are your specific career aspirations?
- Where do you see your graduate training taking you in terms of career options?
- What do you expect to get out of graduate school – how will graduate school change the way you look at the world?

- What are your hobbies and interests outside of psychology? (Be specific: novels read, adventures you have recently experienced, particular hobbies you enjoy.)

Q80. What kinds of questions should I ask in the interview?

A80. You will want to ask questions that reveal that you have done your homework in preparing for the interview and avoid questions to which you should already know the answer such as "What are the required courses?" "How much research will I have to do?" or "Does the Master's program have a thesis requirement?"

Here's a short list of questions that you may find relevant to ask during your interviews:

- How soon will I be able to become involved in research?
- What kinds of financial assistance does your department have for graduate students? Are funds available for professional travel to conferences?
- What is the procedure your department uses for having graduate students select their major professor?
- How long does it take most of your students to complete their degree?
- Are graduate students permitted to participate in departmental activities – do they attend faculty and program meetings, do faculty treat graduate students as junior colleagues?
- What sorts of computer and other technical support are available for graduate student research, including thesis and dissertation work?
- What sorts of jobs have recent graduates of your program been successful in obtaining?

If you are applying to clinical psychology programs or programs that have an applied emphasis, you may wish to ask:

- What kinds of assistantships or practica are available to develop my clinical (or other) skills? What type of clinical supervision is available? What sorts of clinical populations are available locally? How soon before I will begin my clinical assistantship or become involved in clinical practica?

Once again, avoid asking questions to which you already know the answer – they are not helpful in learning what you need to know about the school and program at which you are interviewing.

Q81. Will I be able to talk to graduate students at the interview? If so, what kinds of questions should I ask them?

A81. You will very likely talk to graduate students during your interview. Some useful questions to ask include the following:

- What are the faculty expectations of graduate students?
- How do the faculty treat the graduate students?
- What is the course reading load like?
- What kinds of research, teaching, or clinical/field experiences are available to graduate students?
- How do the students within the graduate program get along?
- Are there any "unwritten" rules in the department?

Graduate students are often asked by program faculty to provide evaluations of the applicants who visit campus. So, remember, even when you think you are free to relax, such as being at a party with only graduate students and the other applicants (no faculty), you are still being interviewed! Evaluate their reactions to your questions as well as their answers. Seeing how comfortable the graduate students are in talking with you about these issues will reveal the kinds of colleagues that you will have should you be accepted and decide to attend that particular school.

One of the most important issues to learn about during the interview is the extent to which faculty treat graduate students like junior colleagues. The extent to which students and faculty are on a first-name basis and the degree to which graduate students are actively involved in departmental committees are often indicative of how much respect faculty have for graduate students.

Q82. Should I write a "thank you" letter to the admissions committee following the interview?

A82. Although it is not necessary to send a thank you letter, it would certainly convey a sense of professionalism that may make a difference in whether you get accepted to graduate school. Be specific in your letter about what you found impressive about the interview, the graduate program, the current graduate students, and the campus.

Chapter 7
Getting In or
Not Getting In:
Reality Strikes

Will your long hours of diligent study and meticulous preparation to enter graduate school pay off? You won't know for sure until you receive that letter or phone call from a member of the admissions committee. If you are accepted to graduate school, the really hard work is just about to begin. If you are not accepted, don't give up – with some extra effort and slight modifications of your original plan, you may still be able to find another way to open the door to graduate school. The questions and answers in this chapter deal with how and when you will be informed about the admissions committee's evaluation of your application, financial aid and assistantship possibilities, and a course of action you may wish to follow if you are not accepted into a graduate program.

Q83. When will graduate programs let me know if I have been accepted?

A83. Most graduate programs extend offers to their top applicants by April 1 (APA requires that graduate programs in clinical or counseling psychology extend their offers by April 15). However, because several schools may extend an offer to the same applicant and because that applicant can only attend one graduate program, slots may continue to open during the remainder of the spring and in some cases into the early summer. Occasionally, an accepted applicant decides not to go to graduate school at the last minute (i.e., just before the fall term begins) and a slot may open up then.

Graduate admissions committees usually divide their applicants, formally or informally, into three tiers: a set of top-choice applicants, waiting-list applicants, and applicants who will not be accepted. Because many schools do not get all of their top choices, they often extend offers to those applicants at the top of the waiting list.

Q84. What should I do if I have not heard whether I have been accepted at a program?

A84. If you have not learned whether your application has been accepted or rejected by mid-April, you should contact each of the programs to which you have applied and inquire as to the status of your application. If a school informs you at that point that your name has been placed on the waiting list, let them know immediately, and in writing, whether you are still interested in attending that program. If your application has been rejected at all the programs to which you have applied and you still wish to attend graduate school, turn immediately to the APA's *Graduate Study in Psychology* (http://www.apa.org/books/4270089.html) and search for programs that have admissions criteria that you know you definitely meet. Contact those programs immediately and inquire if they are still accepting applications. If so, then apply.

Q85. If I am admitted to a graduate program, but cannot start graduate school in the term required, can I arrange to start during a later term?

A85. The answer to this question depends upon the graduate program to which you have been accepted. Some programs are flexible on this point, others are not. In emergency situations, such as a sudden illness, a death in your family, the birth of your child, graduate programs are usually very flexible. However, if the problem with starting during the usual term is simply a matter of personal convenience for you, graduate programs are generally less accommodating. In some cases, you may arrange to defer your start by one year.

Q86. What kind of financial aid is available to graduate students?

A86. The primary forms of financial aid for graduate students include teaching assistantships, research assistantships, scholarships, fellowships, and tuition waivers. Additionally, it is not unusual for graduate students to apply for Stafford Loans to offset the cost of graduate school. But, remember, you have to pay back Stafford Loans.

Many PhD programs will offer teaching assistantships as a part of enrolling in their programs. These assistantships usually require students to be full-time and are limited in number. Additionally, you may become associated with a faculty member who is conducting extramurally funded research (under a grant). You may have the opportunity to work as a research assistant under this faculty member and receive a salary from the grant. In most cases, this faculty member may also serve as your major professor. Your thesis and dissertation may be funded in part by the grant.

If you wish to receive a fellowship, you will need to research and apply for them on your own – start early, preferably during the fall of your junior year of undergraduate school. Fellowships award yearly stipends to outstanding graduate students to conduct their own research under the supervision of a sponsor, usually your major professor. If you are interested in such fellowships you should consult the following publications: *The Foundation Directory*, *Foundation Grants to Individuals*, *Selected List of Fellowships Opportunities and Aids to Advance Education*, and *Don't Miss Out*. The first two are available from the Foundation Center. For more information on these publications, write or call:

The Foundation Center
79 Fifth Avenue
New York, NY 10003
800-424-9836
http://fdncenter.org/

The last two are published by the National Science Foundation. For information about National Science Foundation Fellowships in the social sciences write:

NSF Fellowship Office
National Research Council
2101 Constitution Ave. NW
Washington, DC 20418
703-292-5111
http://www.nsf.gov/

You may also wish to consult the following Web site to find potential sources of support described on the Internet: http://www.graddiv.ucr.edu/ HowFindMoney.html

Q87. When will I find out what my assistantship responsibilities will be?

A87. A description of your assistantship responsibilities is usually sent to you in your letter of acceptance. The description will include a list of your specific duties, the number of hours you are required to work (for example, at many schools, one-third time = 13 hours; half time = 20 hours), your salary, and your faculty supervisor.

Make sure that you know when your assistantship duties begin and when you will receive your first paycheck. Many first-year graduate students have been taken aback because they didn't realize that they would not receive their first paycheck for a month or so after their first term in graduate school had begun!

Q88. From how many different sources am I allowed to receive financial assistance?

A88. Most graduate schools do not place a limit on the number of sources from which you may receive financial assistance. However, some fellowship and loan programs and assistantships do not allow you to receive financial support from other sources. When applying for financial assistance, be sure to raise this question with the funding source or agency.

Q89. Are there employers who will pay for their employees to go back to school and work on their Master's degree or PhD?

A89. Yes, some employers, including some governmental agencies, will pay some or all of the tuition and fees associated with earning a Master's or PhD. If you work, check with your employer about this issue.

Q90. Is housing provided for graduate students?

A90. The vast majority of graduate programs expect their students to find their own housing. Make sure you begin to think about your housing arrangements soon after you are accepted to graduate school. If you wait too long, you may be out of luck when school starts. Your best bet is to make a visit to the campus of your graduate school in the spring or early summer to begin your apartment hunting. The APA *Guide to Graduate Study in Psychology* (http://www.apa.org/books/4270089.html) provides information about housing for each graduate program it describes.

Q91. If I am not admitted to a doctoral program, can I reapply to the same program at a later date?

A91. Yes. However, you were probably denied acceptance the first time because of a low GPA, low GRE scores, or both. Before you reapply, you may first wish to obtain a Master's degree (if you don't have one already), which will give you a chance to raise your GPA and establish that you are capable of doing quality graduate-level work. Depending on how low your GRE scores were the first time you took it, you may consider taking the GRE over again in an attempt to raise your score.

Chapter 8
The First Year:
Thriving, Surviving,
and Other Essentials

As exciting as it is to begin graduate school, for most students, the first year is the most difficult. After all, you will be reading, writing, and otherwise studying more than at any time in your education thus far. After you have survived the first year, you know that you can survive just about anything that the subsequent years of graduate school may throw at you. The questions and answers in this chapter are intended to provide you with a glimpse of some of the decisions and issues that you will face during your first year of graduate school.

Q92. Will I have an opportunity to teach while I am working on my Master's degree? While working on my PhD?

A92. Different graduate programs offer their graduate students different kinds of teaching opportunities. Some programs offer no teaching, at others you might become a Graduate Teaching Assistant, and at some schools you might be totally responsible for teaching a course (usually a lower level undergraduate course). One of the questions you should ask during your interview or visit to campus is whether you will have an opportunity to teach while working on your degree. The majority of graduate students are extremely pleased with the opportunity to teach because of the many skills they acquire while learning to become good teachers. For example, our students have commented on these skills as being especially valuable: public speaking, decreased anxiety of public speaking, knowledge of course content, interpersonal and social skills related to explaining ideas and concepts in one-on-one situations, and skills related to organization and time management.

Q93. Am I free to change my declared area of specialization during graduate school?

A93. As long as you stay within the bounds of your graduate program, you usually can change your area of specialization. For example, if you are a student in an industrial/organizational program you may decide that you are more interested in leadership issues than in personnel issues. Such a change, of course, will be facilitated if there is a faculty member in your program who is also interested in leadership issues and who therefore can serve as your major professor.

Making a change from one graduate program to another within the same department is more difficult and often discouraged, if not disallowed. For example, many psychology departments will not permit graduate students to jump from one program, such as experimental, to another, such as clinical.

Do not think that you can enter a particular graduate program through the "back door." For example, suppose you are denied admission to a clinical program but admitted to the experimental program within the same psychology department. The chances that you can switch from the experimental to the clinical program after you have been in graduate school are not high, and in many psychology departments, your chances are nonexistent.

Q94. When do I choose a major professor?

A94. You will most likely select a major professor sometime during the middle to end of your first year of graduate school. If you wait too long, you'll get a late start on working on your thesis or dissertation, which puts you at a disadvantage in terms of finishing your graduate work in a timely fashion. The earlier you select a major professor (and he or she agrees to serve in that capacity) the sooner you will benefit from the advice and counsel of a mentor. However, you don't want to be in a hurry to select a major professor – you want to take the time to make a wise decision – one that will maximize your chances of selecting someone whose research interests and interpersonal style are compatible with your needs for supervision.

Q95. Should the person I ask to be my major professor be a full professor?

A95. No, your major professor should not be selected according to his or her rank. Rather, you should select a major professor based upon his or her expertise in an area that you, too, aspire to become expert in, and how well you believe you can work alongside him or her.

Q96. What should I look for in choosing a major professor?

A96. Selecting a major professor is one of the most important decisions you will make in your graduate school career. You should not make this decision lightly. Many times graduate students will choose a major professor only to find that they have made an unwise decision. At that point, you'll need to search for a new major professor, possibly change your area of research, and, in the worst case, apply to other graduate programs if you cannot find a new major professor at your current school. Listed below are six issues that you should consider when selecting your major professor:

- Become familiar with the research, theoretical orientations, and personalities of as many of the graduate faculty as you can. Make appointments to visit with them to discuss graduate school, their approach to being a major professor, their ideas on how theses and dissertations should be conducted, their own career goals, and their academic values. Gathering this sort of information is the first step in making an informed decision.
- You should have similar research interests as the graduate faculty member with whom you wish to work. Your major professor should have rigorous methodological standards for his or her own research and have an active research program in the area in which you wish to conduct your research.
- You should be able to get along with your major professor. Although you should not expect to become friends with your major professor, you should be able to develop a close working relationship with him or her so that you will be able to discuss important and personal issues related to your professional development. *Your major professor will be the primary individual who will shape the character of your early career. Select a major professor whose judgment about your professional development you can trust and who will go to bat for you before the other faculty should the need arise.*
- The major professor you select should have the resources necessary for you to conduct research. These resources may include laboratory

space, funds to pay subjects or research assistants, or access to special populations of subjects or off-campus facilities, such as those found in business, industry, and clinical settings. Selecting a major professor who does not have these sorts of resources can severely impede your progress through your graduate program.

- You should choose a major professor who has a good track record with past and present graduate students in the program. This reputation would include the professor's history of being fair and honest with graduate students, treating graduate students as junior colleagues rather than "gophers" or "lackeys," helping graduate students develop good ideas for their theses and dissertations, and seeing that they finish their work in a timely fashion.

- Consider whether you wish to have your committee chaired by a tenured or nontenured professor. There are advantages to either choice. Nontenured faculty are more likely than tenured faculty to leave the department for another job. You may not want to find yourself in a situation in which you are working very hard on your thesis or dissertation only to have your major professor suddenly leave. If your major professor leaves, you'll be without a strong voice to represent you or otherwise support you before the graduate faculty. And, to be sure, long distance student–faculty relationships are very difficult to manage – so don't think that completing your research in a timely or expert fashion will be easy if your major professor moves. On the other hand, nontenured faculty are often extremely hard workers who are looking for ambitious graduate students to help them establish their research program – after all, they are seeking tenure and one of the "must-dos" in this quest is to generate a strong publication record. By working with an untenured faculty member, you may find yourself building a lab from scratch and/or being a coauthor on several research papers early in your graduate career, both of which are extremely insightful learning experiences. (We do not imply that tenured faculty are not hard workers; most are. However, the pressure to become tenured is an incredibly effective mechanism that is often instrumental in motivating young assistant professors to establish and maintain strong, innovative programs of research.)

Q97.   Can I switch major professors during graduate school?

A97.   Yes, you may change major professors, although doing so can often be a delicate matter. If you become unhappy with some aspect of your relationship with your major professor, you should discuss the matter immediately with him or her. For example, you may no longer share his or her research interests or your major professor may not give you the proper amount of attention or otherwise fails to support you. Be honest, but tactful. Graduate faculty typically invest enormous amounts of time and intellectual energy in their graduate students, and they may take your decision to change major professors personally. There is not much you can do about that, except to handle the situation as gracefully as you possibly can. Some major professors may have their feelings hurt because of your decision, but most will not hold it against you.

Q98. When do I choose my thesis or doctoral committee?

A98. Most graduate programs desire that you select a major professor and a thesis committee during your first year of graduate school – and the earlier the better. Waiting beyond the first year to select your committee simply adds that much more time to completing your graduate work. Doctoral committees often contain the same faculty members who served on one's thesis committees. Doctoral committees are officially formed once all requirements for the Master's degree have been met and the student has been granted doctoral candidacy status by the graduate program.

Q99. How many people "wash out" of graduate psychology programs and how can I insure that I will not be one of them?

A99. Only very spotty data exist regarding this question, so we will not attempt to provide a definitive answer here. To prevent yourself from washing out of a graduate program we offer several suggestions:

- Follow the work ethic and work patterns of current successful students in the program. Look to these individuals as role models.
- Make a strong effort to keep your personal life and finances stable – that way they are less likely to distract you in your graduate work and make that aspect of your life unnecessarily difficult.
- Develop strong time-management skills.
- Study and work collaboratively with other graduate students.
- Take your graduate training seriously – graduate school is not simply an extension of undergraduate school. You need to work harder, study longer, and develop exceptionally good verbal and writing skills. Set realistic goals, but be aware that many of your interests

may change during the course of graduate school. Keep an open mind to new ideas.

An absolutely superb resource for discovering and understanding some of the most desirable qualities and characteristics of graduate students may found on the APA Web site at http://www.apa.org/ed howchange.html

This site contains three potentially useful lists of information for any undergraduate contemplating applying to graduate school. The first list describes characteristics that graduate programs like their applicants to possess. The top five characteristics are, in order: (a) motivated and hardworking, (b) strong intellectual and scholarly abilities, (c) strong research skills, (d) emotional stability and maturity, and (e) strong writing skills. The second list is a list of qualities of graduate school "superstars." These highly successful graduate students are: (a) seen frequently in and around the psychology department, (b) hard-working, (c) willing to embrace program and professional values, (d) devoted to working very closely with one or two of their professors, and (e) capable of making their major professor feel valued through hard work, teachability, and productivity. Finally, the third list centers on desirable qualities of undergraduates applying to clinical psychology programs: (a) hard-working, (b) ability to get along with others, (c) writing skills, (d) existing clinical or counseling skills, and (e) research experience. Clearly, the ability to work hard is a key skill found on all three lists, which underscores its critical importance for success in graduate school.

Q100. Should I become involved with extracurricular professional activities (conducting research, attending conferences, working in clinical settings, etc.) during my first year of graduate school?

A100. The answer to this question depends upon the nature of your graduate program. In most programs, students are encouraged to become in-volved in research and attend conferences. Some programs, though, prefer to have students focus on coursework in the attempt to get most of it out of the way during the first year. This point is particularly true of clinical programs where students must satisfactorily complete certain classes before they can be placed in clinical settings for their assistantships during their second year of graduate school. As a general rule, though, the sooner you can become involved in research and attend conferences, the sooner that you will become fully immersed in your profession as it exists in the real world.

Q101. What kind of grades will I be expected to earn during my first year in graduate school?

A101. Most graduate programs expect their students – regardless of how long they have been in graduate school – to earn "As" in all of their courses. "Bs" are acceptable so long as they are occasional. Receiving a "C" in a graduate course is tantamount to failing that course, and most likely you will have to repeat the course in the attempt to earn a "B" or better grade in it. Some graduate programs stipulate that if a student earns two or more "Cs" in courses considered essential to the student's training (sometimes these courses are called "core" courses), then the student is asked to leave the program. In other words, you should try your best to earn an "A" in every graduate course.

Suggested Additional Sources of Information

American Psychologist.
The *American Psychologist* (http://content.apa.org/journals/amp) is published monthly by the American Psychological Association and contains general articles on developments, trends, public policy related to psychology, professional issues within psychology, reviews of different issues and theories, and dates for national and regional APA conferences.

APS Observer and *APA Monitor.*
The *APS Observer* (http://www.psychologicalscience.org/observer) is the official magazine of the Association for Psychological Science and the *APA Monitor* (http://www.apa.org/monitor) is the official magazine of the American Psychological Association. Both magazines contain the latest developments within scientific and professional psychology. They also both contain large employment advertisement sections, which describe hundreds of job opportunities for persons holding Master's degrees and PhDs. The advertisements are listed by state and include both college and university positions as well as openings in the private sector (businesses, hospitals, medical centers, and so on).

Chronicle of Higher Education.
The *Chronicle* (http://chronicle.com/) contains articles of broad interest to college professors across all disciplines. Like the *Observer* and *Monitor*, it contains a large employment bulletin section, which describes job opportunities involving teaching and administrative positions.

Directory of Graduate Training Programs in Behavior Analysis.
Kalamazoo, MI: Association for Behavior Analysis.
This index provides detailed information on behavior-analytic graduate programs, including admission criteria, areas of emphasis, courses,

tuition and fees, GRE information, and interests of program faculty. For general information about behavior analysis or the Association for Behavior Analysis, please see http://www.abainternational.org/

Eye on Psi Chi (http://www.psichi.org/pubs/eye/home.asp).
This magazine is published quarterly by Psi Chi, the national honor society in psychology and is mailed to all active members of Psi Chi. It contains information about student activities at APA and APS national conferences as well as state and local conferences, national and regional student research awards, chapter activities, articles on psychology, and articles related to getting into graduate school.

Getting In: A Step-by-Step Plan for Gaining Admission to Graduate School in Psychology. (1993). Washington, DC: American Psychological Association.
Although now over a decade old, this book still provides accurate general information regarding the application and admissions procedures to graduate school in psychology.

Keith-Spiegel, P., & Wiederman, M. W. (2000). *The Complete Guide to Graduate School Admission: Psychology, Counseling, and Related Professions* (2nd edition). Mahwah, NJ: Lawrence Erlbaum Associates.
This easy-to-read book is an excellent resource for obtaining insightful information about all phases of the application and admission processes as they pertain to psychology and closely related fields.

Kuther, T. (2004). *Graduate Study in Psychology: Your Guide to Success.* Springfield, IL: Charles C. Thomas.
This brief paperback book contains a well-conceived and comprehensive guide to the graduate admissions process in psychology.

Mayne, T. J., Sayette, M. A., & Norcross, J. C. (2006). *Insider's Guide to Graduate Programs in Clinical and Counseling Psychology: 2006/2007 Edition* New York: The Guilford Press.
This book is tailor made for undergraduates who wish to go to graduate school in clinical psychology or counseling psychology. It contains information on clinical and counseling psychology as a profession, preparing and applying to clinical and counseling programs, and research areas, specialty clinics, and practica sites. It also provides detailed information on individual graduate programs, including information on GRE scores, numbers of applicants, women and minority students, specialty areas represented by faculty and numbers of faculty holding grants.

Peters, L. R. (1997). *Getting What You Came For: The Smart Student's Guide to Earning a Master's or a PhD*. New York: Farrar, Straus, and Giroux.
This book is a very well-written and information-rich account of nearly every facet of graduate school – from first contemplating going to graduate school to completing Master's or PhD requirements. This book is not oriented to any one particular discipline; it is directed at students who wish to attend graduate school in any area.

Phillips, E., & Pugh, D. D. (2005). *How to Get a PhD: A Handbook for Students and Their Supervisors* (4th edition). Bristol, PA: Open University Press.
This book is intended to be a compass to help students navigate their way through the hurdles that must be overcome in the quest to obtain the PhD. It details the things a student shouldn't do and offers advice on how to conduct research, how to write the dissertation, how to get along with your major professor, and, in general, how to survive graduate school.

Walfish, S., & Hess, A. K. (eds.). (2001). *Succeeding in Graduate School: The Career Guide for Psychology Students*. Mahwah, NJ: Lawrence Erlbaum Associates.
This volume of essays centers on all aspects of pursing and developing careers in psychology. Its coverage ranges from the academic to social factors that influence excellent performance in graduate school and beyond.

Glossary and Index

ABD (all but dissertation) A term used to describe an individual who has completed all of the requirements for the PhD except the dissertation.

admissions committee A group of several graduate faculty, usually members of the same graduate program, who review completed applications for admission to their graduate program. At some schools, the admissions committee is appointed to represent a larger number of graduate program faculty and at other schools all the members of a graduate program faculty serve as the admissions committee. (Q & A 57, 58)

application materials The materials that constitute an application to graduate school, which typically include your completed application form, a copy of your undergraduate or Master's transcript, your GRE scores, your completed letter of intent, reprints or preprints of completed research, and at least three letters of recommendation. (Q & A 24, 50, 55–71)

APA accreditation The APA's formal approval of a graduate program in psychology certifying that that program has met minimal standards for the training of graduate students in clinical psychology. (Q & A 42)

APA The acronym for the American Psychological Association (see http://www.apa.org/). (Q & A 37, 100)

APA Monitor The *APA Monitor* is the official magazine of the American Psychological Association (see http://www.apa.org/monitor). This publication contains descriptions of the latest developments in both scientific and professional psychology and a large employment advertisement section. It is an excellent resource of information about current issues and trends in psychology.

APS   The acronym for the Association for Psychological Science (see http://www.psychologicalscience.org). (Q & A 100)

APS Observer   The *APS Observer* is the official magazine of the Association for Psychological Science (see http://www.psychologicalscience.org/observer). Like the *APA Monitor*, this publication contains descriptions of the latest developments in both scientific and professional psychology and a large employment advertisement section. It, too, is a bountiful resource of information about current issues and trends in psychology.

area paper   A comprehensive, integrated review paper covering a major area of psychological research. It is not uncommon for the major area paper to be in excess of 100 pages in length. Often the topic discussed in the major area paper is closely related to the topic researched in the dissertation. In lieu of taking the comprehensive and oral examinations, some graduate programs give graduate students the opportunity to write a major area paper and present an oral defense over it. (Q & A 18)

CACREP   The acronym for the Council for the Accreditation of Counseling and Related Educational Programs (see http://www.cacrep.org/).

CAS   The acronym for Certificate of Advanced Study.

CAMPP   The acronym for the Council of Applied Master's Programs in Psychology. Membership in CAMPP is based on a program's application for membership and meeting or exceeding several qualitative criteria (see http://www.camppsite.org/).

comprehensive examinations (also called "comps," "preliminary examinations" or "prelims")   This series of exams covers the coursework during your first two or three years of graduate school, although in some graduate programs these exams are taken after the first year of coursework). These exams are usually each four to eight hours in length and may take up to a week to finish. Passing the exams means that you are promoted to doctoral candidacy, that is, you are allowed to move on in your program to pursue your PhD. In some graduate programs, failing the exams may mean that you are washed out of the program (usually after earning a terminal Master's degree); other programs allow graduate students an opportunity for remediation and a second crack at the exams. However, failing the comprehensive exam twice almost always guarantees expulsion from further graduate work in that program. (Q & A 18)

CRC The acronym for Certified Rehabilitation Counselor.

defense meeting A meeting in which a graduate student orally explains the rationale, methods, findings, and implications of his or her thesis or dissertation to a committee consisting of his or her major professor and two or more departmental faculty. The graduate school usually assigns an "outside reader," a member of the graduate faculty from a different department, to read the dissertation and to be present at the defense meeting. These meetings are often open to the public and attended by other graduate students and faculty. Faculty and others are free to ask questions about any and all aspects of the graduate student's presentation. (Q & A 18)

dissertation A written report of original research conducted by a graduate student in partial fulfillment of the requirements for the PhD. After the dissertation is written, it is defended before the graduate student's dissertation or doctoral committee. (Q & A 18, 19)

dissertation committee A group of graduate faculty members, generally consisting of the graduate student's major professor and two or three other departmental faculty, who supervise the graduate student's dissertation research. The graduate student must defend his or her dissertation before this committee. (Q & A 19, 98)

doctoral candidate A graduate student who has passed all of the requirements necessary to do doctoral-level work. These requirements usually involve satisfactorily completing the Master's degree, finishing required coursework, and passing the comprehensive and oral examinations.

extramural funding (or grant) Funding provided by a nonacademic agency or institution to a faculty member to support research that he or she is conducting. Extramural funding is obtained by writing a grant application, which proposes a series of studies on a particular issue of interest to a given agency or institution, such as the National Science Foundation. On the basis of scientific or practical merit, the committee reviewing the application assigns the application a priority score. If this score is above a certain cut-off point (which varies from time to time), then the granting agency provides the person who wrote the grant funding to carry out his or her proposed research. Many graduate student research assistantships are funded through grants. (Q & A 86, 88)

graduate faculty Members of the faculty who are approved by the graduate school to teach graduate-level courses and to supervise thesis and dissertation research. Graduate faculty are usually active in their fields, frequently publish research, and are competent to teach graduate-level courses. Not all faculty members within a given psychology department are graduate faculty.

graduate program A graduate program is a group of faculty members that is organized around a particular subfield or subdiscipline. The graduate program may establish its own admissions criteria and policies, so long as they meet or exceed the graduate school's criteria and policies. (Q & A 1, 83)

graduate record examination (GRE) The GRE is an aptitude test that is used to assess your academic knowledge and intellectual skills relevant to success in graduate school (see http://www.gre.org). The purpose of the GRE is to provide graduate programs with a quantitative assessment of the applicant's potential to do well in graduate school and that can be easily compared to that of other applicants. The GRE general test is divided into three subtests: verbal ability, quantitative ability, and analytical ability. In addition, there is also a subject test over the prospective graduate student's particular specialty area, in this case, psychology. Most graduate programs require that applicants take only the general test. (Q & A 5, 29, 35, 47–54)

graduate research assistant (GRA) A graduate student who assists a faculty member in conducting research. GRAs are usually paid by the college or university to provide this service as part of their assistantship. GRAs usually work either one-third time (13 hours per week) or half time (20 hours per week). (Q & A 44, 45, 87, 88, 92)

graduate school A graduate school is an administrative body, usually directed by a dean, which establishes general admissions criteria and other policies relating to all graduate programs within a college or university. At most colleges and universities, the application for a particular graduate program is submitted to the graduate school. When the application is complete (application form, letter of intent, GRE scores, transcripts, letters of recommendation, and other materials) the application is forwarded to the appropriate graduate program. (Q & A 1)

graduate teaching assistant (GTA)   A graduate student who assists a faculty member in teaching one or more courses, usually at the undergraduate level. GTAs are usually paid by the college or university to provide this service as part of their assistantship. GTAs usually work either one-third time (13 hours per week) or half time (20 hours per week). (Q & A 44, 45, 87, 88, 92)

helping professional   A person who has been trained to provide medical or mental health services to the public. (Q & A 14)

letter of acceptance   A written document informing a graduate school applicant that he or she has been officially accepted into a graduate program. This letter also contains information regarding the terms of the acceptance and any assistantship information. Letters of acceptance are usually mailed by April 15 of each year. (Q & A 83)

letter of intent   A document written by a graduate school applicant that describes his or her specific interests in psychology, particular skills and strengths acquired during undergraduate school, educational goals and career aspirations, and reasons why the specific graduate program to which he or she is applying is attractive. The letter of intent is sometimes referred to as a "personal statement." (Q & A 64, 65)

letters of recommendation (LOR)   Letters written by faculty who are qualified to comment on an undergraduate's academic and research skills and his or her potential for success in graduate school. (Q & A 5, 65–71)

licensure   To practice psychology, a person generally is required to meet relevant professional criteria specific to the state in which he or she resides and to pass a written examination. After doing so, the person is said to be licensed to practice psychology.

LPC   The acronym for Licensed Professional Counselor.

major professor   A graduate faculty member who chairs a graduate student's thesis or dissertation committee. Graduate students generally work more closely with their major professor than they do with other graduate faculty. Major professors are also sometimes called "major advisors" or "mentors." (Q & A 20, 94–7)

Master's degree   The advanced degree earned by satisfactorily completing a required number of graduate-level courses and usually a thesis (although some Master's degree programs offer a non-thesis Master's degree). Additional coursework, specific written and oral requirements, and the dissertation are required to earn the PhD. (Q & A 16, 17, 21, 22, 25, 26, 34)

MAT   The acronym for the Miller's Analogies Test, a written examination that some graduate programs use for screening applicants to their graduate programs.

mentor   A teacher. In this case, though, a mentor is usually a particular graduate faculty member from whom the student works very closely and learns a great deal. This faculty member is generally the student's major professor. (Q & A 20, 94)

oral examination   An exam that generally is given to a graduate student after he or she has passed the comprehensive examination. The oral exam may last for as long as three hours and may cover the same topics as those covered by the comprehensive exam as well as other topics. The oral exam is given by the dissertation committee. If passed, the graduate student is advanced to the status of doctoral candidacy. (Q & A 18)

PhD (Doctor of Philosophy)   The advanced degree earned by satisfactorily completing a required number of graduate-level courses, certain written and oral requirements, the dissertation, and the dissertation defense. (Q & A 11, 17, 18, 21–6)

proposal meeting   The meeting at which a graduate student proposes the research that will constitute a thesis or dissertation before his or her committee. After hearing the proposal and asking questions to the student about it, the committee offers advice for improving the quality of the research and gives permission for the student to conduct the research. (Q & A 19)

Psi Chi   The national honor society in psychology (see http://www.psichi.org/). Many colleges and universities have Psi Chi chapters that undergraduate students may join, providing that they first meet certain academic standards. Psi Chi chapters are communities of undergraduate students who wish to learn more about psychology as a science and profession and who generally are interested in going to graduate school. (Q & A 6, 35)

PsyD (Doctor of Psychology)   An advanced degree generally pursued by graduates who only wish to practice psychology, usually in clinical settings. The requirements for the PsyD usually place less emphasis on research and more emphasis on application of psychological principles than those for the PhD. (Q & A 23)

rolling deadline   A type of deadline that carries over from one time period to another. For example, many Master's programs review and accept new applications every month, every quarter, or every semester until all slots or positions are filled.

stipend   A sum of money paid at regular intervals to a graduate student for assisting a faculty member in teaching or conducting research. (Q & A 86)

tenure   A special status given to those faculty members who have achieved certain levels of competence in the areas of research, teaching, and service to the field. This status gives faculty a degree of job security not customarily found in private-sector jobs.

tenure-track   A term used to describe faculty positions that involve tenure. Generally colleges and universities hire new PhDs to fill these positions. After a given period, usually five or six years, these persons may apply for tenure.

terminal Master's degree   A Master's degree that is awarded in graduate programs designed for students who will not be continuing on toward their PhD. The term also applies to Master's degrees awarded from graduate programs that award only Master's degrees. (Q & A 8)

thesis   A written report of original research conducted by a graduate student in partial fulfillment of the requirements for the Master's degree. After the thesis is written, it is defended before the graduate student's Master's committee. (Q & A 18, 19)

thesis committee   A group of graduate faculty members, generally consisting of the graduate student's major professor and two or three other departmental faculty, who supervise the graduate student's thesis research. The graduate student must defend his or her thesis before this committee. (Q & A 19, 98)

tuition waiver   The waiver of all tuition and related fees generally associated with taking graduate courses. Many schools offer tuition waivers to attract students and to reduce the cost of attending graduate school. (Q & A 86)

undergraduate research assistant   Undergraduate students who assist faculty in conducting research. Becoming an undergraduate research assistant is one of the best ways to obtain letters of recommendation for graduate school. (Q & A 31–3)

visitation day   The day on which graduate programs invite their top applicants to visit their campus and interview with their faculty. (Q & A 72–81)

vita   A summary or resumé of your academic experiences and credentials. (Q & A 35)

waiting list   The group of graduate program applicants whose credentials, while good, are not quite as impressive as those from "top-choice" applicants. The waiting list is organized by rank, according to the quality of the applications. Applicant's names are placed on the waiting list in the case that one or more top-choice applicants turn down the graduate program's offer. In such a case, the applicants whose names appear at the top of the list are extended an offer. (Q & A 83, 84)

Appendix I
Timetable for Graduate Study Preparation

Freshman Year

- Complete as many general education and core requirements as possible. Earn as high a grade as possible in each course.
- Complete the introductory psychology course and earn an "A" in it. Introduce yourself to the teacher of this course and let him and her know you are interested in pursuing a career in psychology.
- Participate as a subject in psychological research. Participating as a subject will give you a brief look at psychological research and, in some courses, a chance to earn extra credit toward your grade in the class.
- Declare a major in psychology. Study the requirements for the major and design a plan of action to meet those requirements (devise a schedule for completing all required courses and electives that interest you). Soon after you become a psychology major, you will likely be assigned an advisor who will provide valuable counsel to you about courses, research opportunities, graduate school, and career opportunities. Visit your advisor often and keep him or her abreast of your progress in your courses and in preparing for graduate school. Later on, you may ask your advisor to review your vita for suggestions and ideas for improving it. Your advisor will be aware of many graduate programs and may be able to provide you with personal insights about them.

Sophomore Year

- Continue completing general education or core requirements. Earn as high a grade as possible in all of your courses.
- Enroll in other psychology courses. Take lower-level courses that are required for the major and lower-level electives that you find interesting. Earn "As" in these courses. Be sure to introduce yourself to your psychology professors. Drop by and see them during their office hours – discuss with them course topics as well as the kinds of research and writing in which they are engaged. If the research sounds interesting to you, volunteer to serve as an undergraduate research assistant.
- Join Psi Chi (http://www.psichi.org/). Psi Chi is the national honor society in psychology. If your school does not have a local chapter of Psi Chi, it may have a campus psychology club – join it and become an active member. Psi Chi has regular

meetings and schedules other kinds of activities, such as trips to mental health facilities and other psychology-related settings, local conferences and talks, and faculty–student parties. Psi Chi chapters also usually maintain a graduate school resource library and hold study groups for courses. Become an active member and volunteer to help organize Psi Chi functions. The address for the National Office of Psi Chi is:

Psi Chi National Office
PO Box 709
Chattanooga, TN 37401-0709
Phone: 423-756-2044. Fax: 423-774-2443
http://www.psichi.org/

- Begin thinking about a minor. Choose an area that either has direct relevance to your area of interest within psychology or that will serve as a "tool" to help you develop your writing or analytical skills (e.g., English, computer science, mathematics, statistics, philosophy).
- Become aware of and attend local, state, and regional psychology meetings. Attend any talks, colloquia, or symposia sponsored by your psychology department. These events will be wonderful opportunities for you to observe established thinkers and researchers in your chosen field. Often there is a party open to faculty and students following these kinds of presentations. Attend and introduce yourself to the speaker, other students, and faculty.
- Seek out local opportunities for psychology-related volunteer work. Possible settings include: crisis lines, battered women or rape shelters, substance abuse programs, nursing homes, mental health centers, mental retardation centers, and medical centers or hospitals.
- Start reading publications on graduate school. Near the end of your sophomore year, begin to read publications containing information about graduate school. Also, begin to think seriously about possible areas of specialization within psychology. Contact several psychology faculty members to seek their advice and counsel about the areas that interest you.

Junior Year

- Continue volunteer work and research projects. Continue to attend talks, colloquia, and symposia on campus.

- Consult psychology faculty about any summer job opportunities in psychology. Although rare, you may find a part-time job related to psychology that is available through educational institutions, private laboratories, and research funded by faculty grants. The earlier you find out about these positions and apply for them, the better your chances of obtaining psychology-related employment.
- Enroll in upper-level psychology courses, especially those required for the major. Enroll in the statistics and research methods courses early in your junior year if you have not already taken these courses. Work very hard to earn "As" in each of these courses – they will be among the most important undergraduate courses you take in preparation for graduate school. Both courses should be completed before you take the GRE.
- Become actively involved as an undergraduate research assistant. Find faculty members whose research interests are related to yours. These faculty will become good sources for your letters of recommendation for graduate school.
- Meet graduate students. Take advantage of opportunities to discuss graduate student life with the graduate students at your school. Ask them about the types of courses, course workloads, paper requirements, how to get along with professors, financial aid, and thesis and dissertation work. Have them keep you informed about upcoming talks, colloquia, and symposia on campus. If you are attending a college or university consisting of only undergraduates, consult with the psychology faculty to see if they can possibly put you in touch with former students who are now in graduate school.
- Prepare your vita. Use the outline given in Appendix III. Again, remember, the vita is primarily for your own use. Do not include your vita among your application materials unless it is specifically requested by the graduate program to which you are applying.
- Become a student affiliate of APS and APA. Join other organizations, which are related to your areas of interests, as a student member.
- Read the *APA Monitor*, the *APS Observer*, and the *Chronicle of Higher Education*. Scan the employment advertisement sections of these newspapers to gain an idea of the kinds of jobs available to persons graduating with Master's degrees and PhDs in your areas of interest. These publications are likely to be available in your library. If not, ask faculty or graduate students if you can borrow their copy.

- Register for the GRE. During the fall of your junior year register for the GRE that will be given in the spring. Purchase and use the study guide and software available for practicing for the GRE. Taking the GRE in your junior year leaves you room to take it over again should you do poorly on it the first time. If you decide to take the GRE over again, register for it as soon as possible.
- Purchase a copy of the APA's *Guide to Graduate Study in Psychology*. (Do so during the fall of your junior year.) Study it carefully, noting those graduate programs that most interest you. Be sure you also note the kind of GPA and GRE scores that you need to earn to be competitive for those programs.
- Request information from graduate programs either through the Internet or regular mail. During the spring of your junior year, request those graduate programs that most interest you to send you an application, school catalog and other information describing program details. After receiving these materials, study them carefully – you'll need to determine exactly what you need to do to complete applications for each program during the late summer of your junior year and fall of your senior year. Be sure that you request each graduate program to send you information regarding assistantships, fellowships, and tuition waivers available through their program. Also seek information about scholarships, fellowships, and loans that may be available through other sources.
- Prepare for the GRE Psychology Subtest. During the summer of your junior year, prepare for taking the advanced subject GRE subtest. Purchase and use the study guide and software available to practice for this subtest. Register to take the quantitative and verbal subtests over again (if necessary) and the Psychology Subtest no later than October. If you must, register to retake the entire GRE in December.
- Visit the campuses of those graduate schools in which you are most interested in attending. Such visits permit you to learn first-hand the nature of the campus and graduate program and to make acquaintance with graduate faculty. Another advantage of such visits is that you may find that your relative preference for graduate programs changes as you meet faculty and tour their working environment. You may wish to schedule visits to your most preferred graduate schools during the late summer of your junior year or early fall of your senior year.

Senior Year

- Choose faculty to write your letters of recommendation.
  Determine in the early fall of your senior year which faculty
  members will write you the best letters of recommendation.
  Give each faculty member an updated copy of your vita when
  you ask them to write your letter. Also give them the following
  information and items:

  - Any application or letter of recommendation form.
  - Any graduate program descriptions.
  - Deadline dates for each application.
  - A stamped envelope addressed to each graduate program.

- Give each faculty member at least four to six weeks to write
  your letter. About 10 days before each deadline, you should
  contact each of your letter writers to ensure that your letters
  have been sent or are in the process of being sent.
- Obtain copies of your transcripts. Make sure you get transcripts
  from every institution of higher learning that you have attended.
  Check each transcript for accuracy; get inaccuracies resolved
  as soon as possible.
- Prepare photocopies of your vita and other application materials. Arrange to have transcripts sent to the graduate schools to
  which you are applying as soon as your fall term grades can be
  included in them.
- Make sure you arrange to have your GRE scores sent to the
  graduate schools to which you are applying.
- Apply to graduate programs. During the early to middle of the
  fall, apply to those graduate schools that have programs most
  likely to satisfy your interests and needs. Be sure to apply to
  "backup" schools should you not get accepted at your first
  choice.
- Check your graduation status. Early in your senior year, check
  with the registrar's office or dean's office to make certain that
  you have taken all of the general education and other courses
  required for your baccalaureate degree.
- Check and recheck that your application materials have been
  sent. Near the end of the fall term of your senior year, recheck (by
  making the appropriate phone calls or personal inquiries) that
  all applications materials have been sent to the schools to which
  you are applying – especially your letters of recommendation.

- Verify receipt of your application materials. In January, contact each graduate program to which you have applied and inquire as to whether all of your application materials have been received. Any materials that have not been received must be submitted right away.

Appendix II
General Concentrations of Psychology in Graduate School

Psychology is an incredibly diverse discipline; it touches upon every aspect of human life. To be sure, if there is a behavior in which humans engage, there is a subdiscipline of psychology that studies it. The list of concentrations in psychology that appear below is intended to provide you with a general overview of some of the most popular and active areas of study in psychology today.

behavior analysis   The study of the relation between behavior and its consequences. Behavior analysts may be basic researchers and affiliated with experimental psychology programs at colleges and universities. Other behavior analysts are interested in specific applied issues, for example, classroom management, mental retardation, autism, personal and employee safety, and organizational behavior. Applied behavior analysts may be found working both in academic settings, such as in the classroom and laboratory, and in private or governmental settings, such as mental health centers and private industry. Currently, the job market is better for applied behavior analysts than basic or experimental behavior analysts.

clinical psychology   Clinical psychology is a broad, diverse field that encompasses many kinds of therapeutic settings. Most clinical psychologists are interested in the application of psychological principles to specific types of mental disorders, such as depression, schizophrenia, or obsessive-compulsive disorders, although some deal strictly with people who have problems adjusting to everyday life situations. Many clinical psychologists may be found in academic settings, serving as teachers and researchers. However, many more are found in private practice, mental health, and medical centers providing psychological services. Clinical psychologists generally specialize in either child, adolescent, or adult clinical psychology. The job market traditionally has been very good for clinical psychologists. It is not uncommon to find clinical psychologists who work full-time for a college or university and who work part-time in a clinic or private practice.

cognitive psychology   The study of cognitive processes, such as thinking, perceiving, imagining, and remembering. Cognitive psychologists are most likely found working in academic settings as teachers and researchers. Within experimental psychology, more jobs have been available recently for cognitive psychologists than for other kinds of experimental psychologists.

counseling psychology   Counseling psychologists are most often trained in departments of counseling psychology. Like clinical psychologists, counseling psychologists may be found in academic settings or in private practice or clinical settings. The job market for counseling psychologists has traditionally been very stable.

developmental disabilities   Persons working in the area of developmental disabilities are most often found working with the staff of mental health and mental retardation facilities and with persons who are mentally retarded, autistic, or who suffer from some other developmental disability. Most often developmental disabilities specialists work within state systems of mental retardation or serve as consultants to those systems. Because mental retardation has long been neglected, there are many career opportunities in this area of applied psychology.

developmental psychology   The study of behavioral, cognitive, emotional, perceptual, and social growth and maturation over the course of the life-span. Developmental psychologists generally specialize in one aspect of development, such as childhood, adolescence, or adulthood. Developmental psychologists also generally work within academic settings as teachers and researchers, although many may work as consultants to child-care facilities, teen organizations, and nursing homes and geriatric centers. The job market for developmental psychologists, like other types of academic psychologists, is highly competitive.

educational psychology   Educational psychologists are interested in all aspects of the interaction that takes place among students, teachers, school administrators, and parents. In general, educational psychologists work to develop teacher training programs, develop selection criteria for teachers, counsel students with school-related problems, design curricula, and develop and implement programs to increase student learning and student motivation. Educational psychologists focus primarily on instructional design and issues related to curricula and classroom issues. Educational psychologists are usually trained in departments of education where they may receive the Masters of Education and/or the Doctor of Education (EdD).

evolutionary psychology   Evolutionary psychologists study the adaptive nature of behavior. They are particularly interested in how inherited dispositions have evolved and how they aid organisms in surviving. Evolutionary psychology is a relatively new field that recognizes that genetics exert at least some control over many human behaviors. Evolutionary psychologists are primarily employed in academic settings and are often trained as experimental psychologists or neuroscientists with specializations in evolutionary theory, genetics, and behavior.

experimental psychology   Experimental psychology is the general name for the combined study of research methods, statistics, and any particular subdiscipline of psychology, such as behavior analysis, cognitive psychology, developmental psychology, or social psychology. Experimental psychologists, then, are trained to apply specific research methods and statistical analyses to their chosen specialty area. The job market for experimental psychologists varies depending upon the specialty area.

forensic psychology   Forensic psychology is the application of psychological principles and theories to the law and justice system, especially as they pertain to criminal behavior and crime solving. Forensic psychologists are often called upon by law enforcement agencies and the court to provide assistance in compiling criminal profiles, analyzing a criminal's psychological history with respect to abnormal behavior, and serving as expert witnesses in court.

human factors/engineering psychology   Human factors psychology studies how humans behave when working with machines in work settings. Human factors psychologists are primarily interested in how to improve human–machine interactions in terms of increasing work efficiency, safety, and productivity. With new technology emerging every day, this branch of psychology has a promising future. Human factors psychologists are employed in both university settings and in private industry. They are often trained as experimental psychologists or industrial/organizational psychologists with an emphasis in computer science, cognitive science, and engineering.

industrial/organizational (I/O) psychology   The study of the relationships between people and their work. I/O psychologists research topics and issues such as employee selection, job performance, placement, training and development of specific skills, organizational structure, employee motivation, and leadership. They also develop and evaluate tests for personnel selection, employee training, job satisfaction, and employee productivity. Although some I/O psychologists may be self-employed as consultants, many others work in business, government, and educational settings. In the past several years, employment opportunities for I/O psychologists have been excellent.

legal psychology   Legal psychologists study every facet of the legal system including defendant and victim characteristics in relation to jury decisions, jury selection, jury decision-making processes, police interrogation strategies, police line-up strategies, eyewitness testimony, expert witness testimony, and many other topics. Legal psychologists are often employed by law firms as consultants. They are also employed in universities where they conduct research. Legal psychologists are often trained as experimental social psychologists and often have additional training in the law.

personality psychology   Personality psychology is the study of the behavior patterns of individuals that remain stable for prolonged periods. Personality psychologists typically attempt to identify specific behavioral, cognitive, and emotional patterns that are characteristic of certain groups of people. (These patterns are called personality types.) Personality psychologists are typically employed in university settings and may be trained as either experimental or clinical psychologists.

psychiatry   Psychiatrists are medical doctors who have expertise in the medical treatment of psychological disorders. Their primary responsibilities include the prescription of medication for those disorders and the monitoring of the patient's treatment.

psychometrics   The study of tests and measurements. Psychometricians develop and evaluate questionnaires, inventories, and other tests specific to a particular dimension or characteristic of behavior and thought. Their main interest is the development of measures of psychological phenomena such as happiness, self-control, depression and other mental disorders, and marital satisfaction that are reliable and valid. Usually psychometricians are extremely well trained in statistics and research methodology. Psychometricians are hired to work in a tremendous array of settings, including political forecasting organizations and think tanks, governmental agencies, polling organizations, business and industry, mental-health settings, and colleges and universities.

neuroscience   Neuroscience is the study of the relationship among genetics, the brain, the nervous system, the endocrine system, and behavior. It represents the integration and collaboration of many biological fields, such as genetics, pharmacology, and cell biology, among others. Of all the scientific fields comprised by psychology, this area is probably the hottest field and will be likely to stay that way for some time. Job opportunities in this area are becoming more numerous, although extremely competitive.

psychopharmacology   Psychopharmacology is a branch of psychology that studies the behavioral effects of drugs in humans and other animals. Psychopharmacologists are typically employed in university or hospital settings conducting research or in private industry (pharmaceutical companies) conducting research on new drugs. Psychopharmacologists often are trained as experimental psychologists and have expertise in biological psychology, behavior analysis, and pharmacy.

school psychology   School psychologists concentrate mainly on testing (psychometrics) and counseling issues. Like educational psychologists, school psychologists are usually trained in departments of education where they may receive the Masters of Education and/or degree of the Doctor of Education (EdD).

social psychology   The study of interactions among people in groups of all sizes. Social psychologists study how groups function to influence the behavior of their members and others who come into contact with them. Social psychologists also study specific psychological processes such as interpersonal attraction; social cognition and perception; gender, ethnic, minority, and political issues; discrimination; prejudice; and group decision-making. In fact, there is probably not a dimension of modern social life in which you can't find a social psychologist or two who is a specialist in it. Social psychologists are most often found teaching and conducting research in academic settings, although they are found in increasing numbers in governmental agencies, business and industry, and private research settings.

sports psychology   Sports psychologists are interested in how psychological factors affect athletic performance. Team cohesion, pre-competition anxiety, mental rehearsal, motivation, and athlete personality characteristics are all among the topics that sports psychologists might study. Many sports psychologists are trained as clinical psychologists who specialize in some facet of sports psychology. Sports psychologists are typically employed in private practice, in consulting firms that consult with professional sports teams, or in universities where they teach and conduct research.

Appendix III
Outline for the Vita and
Sample Vita

Outline for the VITA
(Your name and date)

Biographical Information
Address:
Phone Number(s):
E-mail Address:

Educational and Career Objectives
(In two to three lines, state a specific area of interest and what your goals are with respect to that area)

Education
(College or University only)
Identify Major and Minors:
Overall GPA:
Psychology GPA (List psychology courses taken to date and grades in each)
Composite GRE Score: Verbal: Quantitative:

Honors and Awards
(Psi Chi, honors program, student and civic awards, relevant extracurricular activities)

Memberships in Professional/Scholarly Organizations
(Name organization and indicate any leadership positions you may have held)

Research Experience
(Describe the experience, list duties, name supervisor)

Teaching Experience
(Describe the experience, list duties, name supervisor)

Clinical/Professional/Volunteer Work Experience
(Describe the experience, list duties, name supervisor)

Published Research
(Authors' names, year published, paper title, journal name, volume number, page numbers [Use correct APA format])

Presentations at Scholarly Meetings
(Includes posters and oral presentations): (Authors' names, title of presentation, meeting name, date of meeting [Use correct APA format])

References
(Names, titles, addresses, telephone numbers, and e-mail addresses)

Note: After you have created a vita, make sure to update it with any new information regarding your accomplishments. For example, immediately after you present a poster (which is not already listed on your vita), you should add the relevant information concerning it to your vita.

Sample VITA

Cody N. Sierra
(July 19, 2006)

Biographical Information

Address:	249 Kingfisher Lane
	Wesser, NC 27546
Phone Number(s):	334 555 5292 (H)
	334-555-6869 (O)
E-mail:	sierrac@sunc.edu

Educational and Career Objectives

To obtain a PhD in clinical psychology. I wish to specialize in child clinical psychology, particularly the study of childhood anxiety. My career goals center on becoming employed in a university or medical center setting.

Education

Bachelor of Science, Expected June, 2007
State University of North Carolina

Major:	Psychology	GPA:	3.88
Minors:	English:	GPA:	3.79
	Philosophy:	GPA:	4.00
Overall GPA:	3.67		
A	P201	Introductory Psychology	
A	P223	Developmental Psychology	
A	P302	Quantitative Analysis	
A	P303	Research Methods	
A	P304	History of Psychology	
A	P351	Learning	
B	P352	Physiological Psychology	
B	P353	Sensation and Perception	
A	P354	Cognitive Psychology	
A	P414	Social Psychology	

A	P415	Personality
A	P416	Abnormal Psychology
A	P417	Health Psychology
A	P590	Independent Study (Three times)
A	P595	Child and Adolescent Therapy

GRE Composite Score (V + Q) = 1210   V = 620; Q = 590;
Subject: 680

Honors and Awards

Psi Chi
Outstanding Junior in Psychology, 2005

Memberships in Professional Organizations

Student Affiliate, American Psychological Association
Student Member, Association for Psychological Science

Research Experience

For two terms (Fall and Spring, 2005), I have served as a research assistant working on a project investigating the effects of chronic stressors, including family conflict, poverty, and abuse on the development of depression among adolescents living in inner city areas. My responsibilities included scoring video tapes, entering the coded data into a computer program for data analysis, and interviewing some of the adolescents. Investigator: Dr. Connie Park.

Last term I also served as a research assistant on a study involving employer–employee relationships (Spring, 2005). The purpose of this study was to learn more about how the employer–employee relationship influences employee productivity and happiness. My responsibilities included field testing two different questionnaires (I interviewed over 30 workers in a furniture factory), encoding data, entering the data into a computer program, and graphing the results. Supervisor: Dr. Douglas Pruitt.

Clinical/Professional Work Experience

During the past two years, I have served as a volunteer in the following organizations:

Wesser Teen Crisis Line: I received phone calls from teenagers who had problems with school, their parents, drugs and alcohol, personal relationships, and the law. Supervisor: Lisa R. Shipley

Poplar Nursing Home: I assisted the Home's Recreational Director in organization and carrying out weekend activities for the residents. Supervisor: Joseph Smith.

Nantahala Women's Shelter: I assisted two counselors in working with victims of physical abuse who sought safety in the shelter. Counselor: Dr. Leana Sanchez.

Presentations at Scholarly Meetings

Park, C., Patton, R., & Sierra, C. N. (2005, May). *Poverty as a risk factor in the onset of childhood depression.* Poster presented at the Southern Psychological Association Convention, Orlando, FL.

Sierra, C. N., & Pruitt, D. (2005, October). *On the relation between personnel relationships and job satisfaction.* Poster presented at the American Association for Psychology Conference, Boone, NC.

References

Dr. Connie Park
Psychology Department
State University of North Carolina
Wesser, NC 27546
704-555-1290
e-mail: parkc@sunc.edu

Dr. Douglas Pruitt
Psychology Department
State University of North Carolina
Wesser, NC 27546
704-555-1267
e-mail: pruittd@sunc.edu

Dr. Nancy L. Harte
Chair,
English Department
State University of North Carolina
Wesser, NC 27546
704-555-1282
e-mail: harten@sunc.edu

Note: In addition to serving as a good example of a strong under-graduate vita, this sample vita illustrates four other noteworthy points.

1 Although Cody desires to specialize in the areas of childhood depression and schizophrenia, not all of her research experience (or any of her clinical/professional) experience falls in this area. The important point is that quality research experience as an under-graduate is important by itself – it does not have to be in your stated area of interest to lend strength to your application.
2 Because Cody did not have any teaching experience or any published research, these categories are omitted from her actual vita.
3 Under Research Experience, Cody not only describes the research with which she assisted, she has also describes her specific duties and provides the name of her supervisor.
4 Not all of Cody's references are psychologists – two are, but the third is an English professor.

Appendix IV
Sample Letters of Intent

Letter One

My interest in psychology was sparked by what I learned about this field in my high school psychology course. After explaining to the class all of the different career opportunities available in psychology, my teacher required the class to identify three areas of psychology that interested us the most. I selected clinical psychology, I/O psychology, and experimental psychology. I chose clinical psychology because at the time I was interested in why some people become depressed or schizophrenic and why others do not. I chose I/O psychology because I was interested in finding ways to make businesses and other organizations run more effectively. And I chose experimental psychology because I was fascinated with the idea that human behavior could actually be studied scientifically.

During my freshman year in college I took introductory psychology and realized that psychology interested me more than my other courses. I took two more classes (developmental psychology and research methods) and realized then that I wanted to have a career in psychology. I declared myself a psychology major and soon began taking as many psychology courses and related classes as I could. Two things happened. The first was that my interest in psychology became even stronger; the second was that I narrowed down my specific career choice to I/O psychology. My undergraduate coursework taught me that I was more interested in leadership, leadership motivation, goal-setting, and decision-making than other topics. In particular, the course I took in Motivation and Emotion and the two I took in I/O psychology (Introduction to I/O psychology and Training and Supervision of Industrial Personnel) convinced me that I would like to conduct research in the area of leadership. I have not yet identified specific topics in the area to research and I am open to suggestions and further study before I commit myself to a single topic. However, I do know that I wish to obtain a PhD in I/O psychology and work in a university setting.

My undergraduate coursework also strengthened my interest in experimental methods. In fact, I was given permission to take a graduate course in research methods and I minored in statistics. I worked three terms with two I/O professors as an undergraduate research assistant. I worked two terms in Dr. Lind's lab on research aimed at discovering the factors that influence college students to decide on one career path over others. Last term, I conducted field research with Dr. Hansen on the variables that lead people to decide to change their career field after having worked at one specific job for at least ten years. At present, I am helping these faculty members prepare poster presentations for APA. I will be third author on both presentations.

In addition to having a solid background in research methods and statistics, I also have strong computer skills. I am competent in using several word-processing systems as well as using several statistical packages. I have a clear sense of the direction I wish my career to take and feel certain that I am capable of successfully completing a PhD program in I/O psychology. I wish to become a graduate student in your program because of its challenging academic standards, the reputation of its faculty, and its strength in the area of leadership and leadership motivation. I hope that you will give my application strong consideration.

Letter Two

My interest in psychology began in my freshman year of college. I had the opportunity to take introductory psychology from the most difficult professor at Carlson University. I excelled in the class and became interested in the study of human behavior. In high school I found the sciences (chemistry, physics, and biology) very interesting but lacking in satisfying my desire to help people. Psychology was the answer. It blended my desire to help people with my interest in science. I wanted to learn how to study human behavior scientifically.

From my freshman year until I received my Bachelor's degree I focused on increasing my understanding and skills in psychology. I took one or two courses in psychology every semester and excelled in all of them. During the summers I tried to find employment in areas that involved helping people. Over three summers I have held summer employment in three different summer camps for children. It was then that I became interested in the development of children. During my senior year in college I took a three-week internship with Sioux Ridge School and observed and participated in two of their programs. For two weeks I served as a counselor at a wilderness camp for boys with severe behavior disorders. During the third week, I worked in a community-based foster-care program. Through this experience I was struck by the children's need for help and how much they could learn, despite their less than adequate upbringing. I also realized that many of the problems experienced by the children in the Ridge's programs were not solely due to their behavior, but were also related to the behavior and their relationships with parents and siblings. After this experience, I decided to pursue an advanced degree in clinical psychology.

There are other important areas of my undergraduate education. The most important has been my research. I took a course in human sexuality during my sophomore year in which the professor required a research report. I conducted survey research correlating college students' religious orientation with their knowledge of human sexuality and sexual permissiveness. In addition to the course requirement, I presented the paper to a Kansas Psi Chi State student paper conference and competition. When I took social psychology I helped conduct a group research project. We studied the effects of finding money in a pay phone on people's willingness to perform altruistic behavior. We planted quarters in change returns of pay phones and then a confederate dropped some personal items (books, shopping goods, etc.) in front of unsuspecting subjects in a local shopping mall. We found that people who had inadvertently found the quarters helped the confederates more often than those who did not find the quarters. Finally, I refined my skills in designing and conducting research after taking a course in experimental psychology and a course in statistics.

There are many areas within clinical psychology that are interesting to me, but I am most interested in the development of children in relation to their family. I am especially interested in studying child psychopathology (especially the treatment of attention deficit hyperactivity disorder (ADHD) and autism), and adolescent development. I am sure there are many areas in clinical psychology to which I have not been exposed, and I look forward to learning more about them in your child clinical psychology program. I am applying to your program in child clinical psychology because of its outstanding reputation and its well-rounded faculty and training in all areas of child development and family systems. I would like very much to attend your program.

Letter Three

I am applying to your experimental psychology program because of its strong, high-quality reputation in the areas of social and developmental psychology and because I wish to work under Dr. Rachel Carr. I am particularly interested in assisting Dr. Carr in her research on social development among young, poverty-stricken children. My ultimate goal in going to graduate school is to learn how to conduct independent research on this and related topics. Although I am extremely interested in Dr. Carr's research, I fully realize that I will be exposed to a wide array of research problems during graduate school and I wish to keep an open mind to the possibility that my research agenda may change. But, for the time being, I am confident in my decision to begin my graduate education focused on social development.

I first became interested in this area during my developmental psychology class, which I took during my sophomore year. We had to write a short research review paper for the class and I chose to write on social developmental differences between poverty-stricken and affluent children. In compiling a bibliography for the paper, I came across some of Dr. Carr's papers in this area. I have now had the opportunity to read all of her work, including her book with Dr. Richard Stone.

During my junior year, I conducted an undergraduate research project under the supervision of Dr. Anne Hartsell. The project involved looking at how diet, health, and environmental history affect female rats' maternal behavior toward their offspring. My responsibilities included breeding the animals, animal care-taking duties, measuring the dependent variables (time spent nursing and grooming the offspring and recording any maternal aggressive behavior toward the pups). We presented the results of this study in a poster at the 2006 Southeastern Psychological Association (SEPA) Convention.

I have continued to work with Dr. Hartsell on research in the area of maternal behavior and I am third author on a paper that has been recently submitted to *Development*. In this research, we injected pregnant rats with several different hormones and then carefully monitored the physical and behavioral development of their offspring (we compared their development to that of other pups whose mothers had been injected with a placebo). I have found my experience in Dr. Hartsell's laboratory extremely satisfying and incredibly challenging. I know that I wish to devote my career to conducting research within an academic environment. Ideally, I would like to both teach and do research in a university setting.

In addition to my interest in research, I am also a hard worker who is highly self-motivated and energetic. I am a quick learner; I read a lot and ask questions. I have been working in Dr. Hartsell's laboratory for almost three years, so I am familiar with computer technology, several statistical and word-processing packages, and preparing data for presentation at meetings or publication in journals. I have strong verbal skills and I am comfortable speaking before others. My writing skills are fair, but steadily improving as I gain more experience in writing term papers and research reports. In short, I am confident in my ability to become a capable graduate student and good representative of your graduate program. I sincerely hope that you will give my application every consideration. Thank you.

CPSIA information can be obtained at www.ICGtesting.com
Printed in the USA
BVOW04s1003130215

387565BV00008B/112/P

9 781405 140522